The Art of
PISHING

By the same author

Pete Dunne's Essential Field Guide Companion

Pete Dunne on Bird Watching

Golden Wings

The Feather Quest

The Wind Masters

Small-headed Flycatcher

Before the Echo

More Tales of a Low-Rent Birder

Tales of a Low-Rent Birder

Hawks in Flight (coauthor)

The Art of
PISHING

How to Attract Birds
by Mimicking Their Calls

PETE DUNNE

STACKPOLE
BOOKS

To Harold Axtell,
who would have been both pleased and amused

Published by
STACKPOLE BOOKS
5067 Ritter Road
Mechanicsburg, PA 17055
www.stackpolebooks.com

Printed in the United States of America

10 9 8 7 6 5 4 3 2 1

First edition

Audio tracks of Pete Dunne recorded and engineered by Thomas Smead, Sound Strike Studios, Marmora, NJ
Photographs by Linda Dunne unless otherwise indicated
Cover photo of Tufted Titmouse by Steve Maslowski and Black-capped Chickadee by Bill Marchel
Cover design by Wendy A. Reynolds

Library of Congress Cataloging-in-Publication Data

Dunne, Pete, 1951–
   The art of pishing : how to attract birds by mimicking their calls / Pete Dunne.— 1st ed.
      p. cm.
   ISBN-13: 978-0-8117-3295-6
   1. Bird attracting. 2. Animal calls. 3. Birdsongs. I. Title.

QL676.5D86 2006
598.072'34—dc22   2006004022

> **WARNING: Reading this book and practicing its tenets could have dire, life-altering consequences. You could be eaten by bears, ostra-cized by your children, or, worse, you could turn into a bird watcher.**

Pishing Becomes Scilly

I t was September 1987. Wife Linda and I were enjoying our second day of birding on Britain's picturesque Scilly Isles. We had already seen many of the more common birds of the region—robin, dunnock, wren (the species that typically festoon greeting cards, coasters, and porcelain objects sold in quaint little stores that reek of potpourri and spell *shop* with an *e*). We were, after the fashion of birders, strolling along the walking trails that knit the pastoral countryside in search of more and different birds.

Breaking into a sunny vale, we were halted by the sound of soft, whistled call notes coming from a brushy edge. The birds that were the source of the calls weren't visible (of course). As a rule, woodland birds aren't vain, aren't reckless, and unless defending a territory or trying to attract a mate, see very little reason to be standing in plain view.

So I offered them a reason.

PusssshEE! PussshE! PussshE! P'PS'PusssshEE! PussshE! PusssshE! . . .

To a human listener, my hissing harangue might suggest a stuttering teapot with a lisp or an old steam radiator having a nervous breakdown. To birds it says: "Whoa! Somebirdy's

1

really hot about something over there. I wonder what's going down in the neighborhood."

But the reserved nature of the English seems to infect the island's birds, too. Although some modest interest was evident (i.e., furtive movement behind the outer foliage) their reaction was more akin to: "Curious, what?" It wasn't the avian onslaught I was hoping for. I tried another trick.

T'o'o'o'o'o'o'o'o'o'w/eO'O'O'O'o'o; w/eO'O'O'O'o'o . . .

I've got to tell you I'm pretty darn proud of my Eastern Screech-Owl imitation, and I'm often surprised at how responsive birds that have no familiarity with this small, nocturnal predator can be. This time it didn't register much more than polite silence.

OK, I thought, let's see how the famed British reserve fares against this.

Bringing two fingers up to my lips, pressing lightly, I filled the glen with series of high, shrill, heartrending squeals.

SKREEEUH . . . SKREEEUH . . . SKREEEUH . . .

The sound replicates the cries I once heard coming from a European Starling protesting the inopportune grip of a very unsympathetic Cooper's Hawk.

That did it. Before you could say Crispin's Day, the hedges were vibrating with tiny olive-backed warblers that added their own voices to my harangue.

"Know what they are?" asked Linda.

"Chiffchaffs or maybe Willow Warblers, I think," I thought (but couldn't say). That's the problem with having two fingers plastered against your lips. You can talk only to birds, and unless you want to break the spell and send them back on their merry way, you have to keep squealing.

SKREEEUH . . . SKREEEUH . . . SKREEEUH . . .

More birds coming in all the time.

SKREEEUH . . . SKREEEUH . . . SKREEEUH . . .

Birds moving closer. Birds dancing in the sunlight. Birds in plain view, offering lots of time for study and appreciation. The key to bird study is intimacy. In order to gain such intimacy, bird-watchers have used bird feeders, which bring birds close, or optics, which make them appear close. In simple fact, pishing is just another way of bringing birds close.

By this time the "mobbing action," as these avian social protest sessions are called, was self-sustaining. The agitated birds were calling in other birds, doing my work for me.

"See anything different?" I asked (between squeals and out of the side of my mouth).

"No. You?"

In fact I did see something different. Out of the corner of my eye. Five British birders, wide-eyed, drop-jawed, and panting hard, staring first at the birds, then at us, then back at the birds.

"It's called pishing,'" I shouted. "Nothing but Willow Warblers so far."

I continued to squeal for a while longer, more for the sake of our newly arrived colleagues than for us, then stopped, breaking off the engagement, letting the birds go back to the serious business of being birds. We continued on in search of other birds, leaving our British acquaintances to work through the birds we'd attracted, which were still much in evidence. As we walked by, they stared. In fact, they appeared awed.

That evening at the Porth Cressa, the pub frequented by the hosts of Scilly Birders, we chanced to find a table (no small miracle in itself) and by fortune found ourselves not far from a small, intense throng of birders surrounding one of the chaps we'd run into in the glen.

And he was telling the story of
"This *amazing* Yank
"Who was making the most *horrendous* noises
"That were driving the Chiffchaffs *mad*.
"Of course," he added, "he didn't have any idea what he was looking at. But it was still the most *amazing* thing."

It is amazing. Even better than that. Anyone can do it.

In the Beginning: Speaking in Tongues

1

On my eighth birthday, my sainted Gran'mither Dunne gave me a book. A *beautiful* book. Leather bound. Gold edged. Embellished with a bouquet of multicolored ribbons that could be used to mark the place of unforgettable passages so you wouldn't have to remember them. The book weighed about as much as I did.

The name of the book was *Lives of the Saints.* It was sort of like a field guide to all the Saintly Greats as recognized by the Roman Catholic Church (an institution that is to the confirmation of saints what the American Ornithologists' Union is to the naming of birds).

Now I'm not going to lie and claim that I actually read this tome. I didn't. But I did study the plates. Depiction after depiction of beatific beings. All kneeling or standing in that classic arms-spread, wide-to-the-side stance of saints. All capped with golden halos, which is the diagnostic field mark of a saint.

Virtually all the saints wore robes. OK maybe one or two were wearing armor, but most wore robes. There was one notable exception. Some guy named St. Francis, a monk (probably a Franciscan monk). This guy was wearing birds.

Out of the mouths of birds and babes . . . The fledgling author gets his first lesson in birdspeak. Clearly, at a very early age, his fate was sealed.
PHOTOGRAPHER UNKNOWN

Birds perched on his shoulders. Birds running down his arms. Birds of every stripe and hue. It looked as though he'd reached into the vestibule that morning and slipped into a full-length aviary.

Now *that*, I remember thinking at the time, is a guy who knows how to attract birds.

That, I thought at the time, would be a trick worth knowing.

It is worth knowing because clearly St. Francis was history's first recorded pisher. And although he probably pished in Latin (as some ornithologists still do today), the results were the same. Pish and the whole pishable avian world comes to you.

But I didn't know the secret, wasn't ken to the Order of Pishers until the fall of 1975, when I met a guy named . . .

"Floyd Wolfarth," he said, standing, offering me his hand.

We were situated atop Raccoon Ridge, one of New Jersey's most celebrated hawk-watching junctions. I was twenty-four, a first-year rookie on the hawk-watching circuit. The guy in front of me looked like Michelangelo's image of God wearing binoculars.

Standing over six feet tall. With a mane of long white hair and a billowing white beard. Brandishing a patrician nose and armed with eyes so blue that they rivaled the heavens. He did, in fact, resemble the biblical figures that festoon the ceiling of Sistine Chapel. Even Floyd's voice had a low rumble that sounded like distant thunder and a constant quality that recalled the unfaltering pounding of waves on the shore.

Yes, it's no small understatement to say that Floyd was a talker and that one of his favorite topics was himself. I quickly learned that he, Floyd P. Wolfarth, was . . .

A founding member of the august Urner Ornithological Club—North Jersey's finest.

The former regional editor for *Records of New Jersey Birds*.

Founder of the Boonton and Walnut Valley Christmas Bird Counts, and (somewhat unofficially) the compiler of the Raccoon Ridge Hawk Count.

And that he, in addition to his many other illustrious accomplishments, had once birded with . . . "The Great One," Roger Tory Peterson himself.

"Rodge," as Floyd called him.

In quick sum, I learned that I was in the presence of a birding deity. As even more evidence of his lofty standing, Floyd could make the birds of the air come at his beck and call.

As we were talking (more accurately, as Floyd was talking and I was listening), a small group of Black-capped Chickadees

The late Floyd P. Wolfarth, retired teamster, birding guru, and one hell of a pisher.

LEONARD LEE RUE III

started leapfrogging along the ridge. Floyd started speaking in tongues.

Pssssh, psssh, psssh; Pssh, pssh, PssssssssEH, psssh, psssh . . .

Now I didn't know what he was saying. But those chickadees sure did, and they didn't like it one bit. Before you could say "holy Paridae" the entire flock had spun around and flown back as if homing in on St. Francis's beckoning hand. They landed in the branches of the stunted hickories all around us. Crouched, hopped, and fluttered to within arm's length, Chicka-*dee, dee, dee*ing in a frenzied, stuttering rage.

I'd just witnessed my first display of pishing.

I'd also just met my mentor.

Pishing: What It Is, What It's Not, Where It Came From

Pishing is an onomatopoeic term applied to a variety of orally produced noises that, in general, mimic the scolding calls of birds. If this is not the definition you had in mind, then you were confusing pishing with something else.

Incidentally, to save you the trouble of running for a dictionary, *onomatopoeia* is the "formation of words in imitation of natural sounds." One example is *buzz*, the sound of the vibrating wings of a fly or bee. Another is *cluck*, the word we use to describe one of the common vocalizations of a chicken.

Pishing is the onomatopoeic recasting of the most basic sound in the pishing repertoire, the *psssh* sound used by Floyd Wolfarth. The label has come to apply, variously, to lots of other sounds that, by themselves or in concert, can be used to attract birds. In this book, when I use the term "pishing," I am mostly referring in the generic sense to the full array of bird-attracting sounds—pishes, squeaks, squeals, chips, and imitations.

What natural sound does *psssh* imitate? Good question, and one that lacks a certifiable answer. This is an arcane art—little practiced and less studied. There is no documented history of pishing or a pishing hall of fame or even a single, scholarly treatment of the subject.

But if I had to guess, and since I've backed myself into this etymological corner I guess I do, I'd say that *pish* or *psssh* most closely resembles the raspy, rising scold of Tufted Titmouse—a small, winsome, gray forest bird with a peaked crest, balefully black eyes, and lots of attitude.

There are several pieces of circumstantial evidence that support the titmouse origin theory.

First, Tufted Titmice are common, easily piqued, and often at the heart of (if not the instigators of) mobbing actions. Early students of birds could not help but notice this bird-concentrating behavior, recognize the opportunity it offered for finding and studying birds, and note which species were the prime and most easily imitated instigators.

Second, Tufted Titmouse is a forest bird. Pishing not only works best among forest birds but is also most useful in that habitat (where birds are often hard to find and harder to approach). A person interested in forest birds would be most likely to develop helpful tricks, so it stands to reason that pishing would have its roots in efforts directed toward the study of forest birds.

Third, even though there are lots of forested places in North America, pishing probably has its roots in the eastern, and probably northeastern, United States. As a technique, pishing is generally more effective in the East than in the West, and unless a tried technique is successful, it doesn't perpetuate itself. Tufted Titmouse is an eastern forest bird.

So while the *psssh* in pishing resembles, to some degree, the scold note of many birds (particularly other titmice and chickadees), my guess is that it was the Tufted Titmouse that put the *psssh* in pishing.

Where did the idea of using vocalizations to attract birds come from? Perhaps, as postulated, from early students of birds who noted the possibility during their observations of mobbing actions. But hunters, including Native American hunters, have used imitations of bird calls to lure birds for centuries—the most obvious of which are duck, goose, and turkey calls. (The squeal call that amazed my British birding friends very closely resembles the sound made by an over-the-counter predator call.)

For many years, bird study and bird hunting were virtually synonymous (John James Audubon, painter and publisher of *Birds of America*, was immensely proud of his hunting prowess), so it's possible that the origin, if not the refinement, of pishing can be traced to techniques developed for hunting.

However the technique was developed, one thing is certain. At times, and in the hands of someone who knows how to use it, pishing can work like magic.

Black and White

Many years ago, I was coleading a birding workshop with a focus on migratory birds. It was mid-September and we were in Cape May, New Jersey, a place whose name is almost synonymous with autumn birding. We, my students and I, were walking down a wide dirt road flanked by woodlands.

The morning had been gratifyingly bird-filled but it was getting on toward midmorning and things had quieted down—meaning that the birds had stopped foraging and were now resting under cover. When we reached a spot that seemed strategic (a place with enough cover so birds would feel comfortable but not so overgrown that they would be blocked from view), I stopped the group. Stepping slightly away and closer to the woodland edge, I started pishing.

The results, even by Cape May standards, were magical. It was the peak of the warbler migration, and Black-and-white Warblers were particularly numerous. In short order, we were virtually enveloped in pish-piqued warblers whose close proximity made binoculars superfluous and whose numbers, if I were brash enough to relate them in this more tempered, warbler-lean age of the world, would brand me a liar.

Oh, all right, it was somewhere between thirty and forty black-and-whites (mostly immature), and if you want to call me befuddled or a liar, be my guest. It was nevertheless an impressive number of birds and an impressive display of pishing's effectiveness, and that is what prompted a question from one of the members of the group.

"Why," she wanted to know, "do they do that?"

"Do what?" I asked.

"Why do they come in to those noises and crowd all around?"

"Altruism," I explained. "The birds are coming in to lend their support to another bird that is confronting what is, potentially, a threat to them all."

"Oh," she said.

"D'oh!" I Say

I offered this less-than-complete answer, first, because I probably believed it at the time, and second, because I didn't have a better one. Both those conditions have been tempered by experience.

There may well be some evolutionary or biological advantage for birds to come to the aid of, say, a noisy forest neighbor whose nest is being assailed by a rat snake (assuming that birds practice reciprocity or form mutual aggression pacts) or to help another neighbor heap verbal abuse on a hunting Cooper's Hawk so that the predatory bird, realizing that its cover has been blown, will quit the area. Yes, mobbing very probably offers forest birds some blanket protection.

But how migrants (who are just moving through an area) might benefit from providing aid and comfort to another bird is less clear to me. I'm also puzzled as to why a chickadee and a Downy Woodpecker will join a Ruby-crowned Kinglet in heaping abuse on a roosting Northern Saw-whet Owl when the effort is going to effect no change—the owl's not going anywhere, and both the chickadee and the woodpecker are going to be snug in their tree cavities before the owl starts hunting.

Several years ago I had the opportunity to meet an Israeli behavioral scientist named Amatz Zahavi. He'd spent years studying a tribal and territorial species of bird called the Arabian Babbler (babblers are most closely related to jays) and we, the members of an international assemblage of ornithologists and birders, were invited to his study site.

Dr. Zahavi was not a big proponent of altruism.

By way of demonstration, the scientist enlisted the services of a small viper, placing it under a shady bush. Then he called in his troop of babblers (they were wild and free-ranging but had a weakness for peanuts). It didn't take long before one of the sharp-eyed birds spied the coiled snake and ran directly to the bush, approaching to less than two feet. The bird leaned forward, opened and drooped its wings, and started to scream at the reptile. All the other babblers (about ten) ran over, crowded around the bush, and did likewise.

"Now why are they doing this?" the scientist asked aloud. If the objective, as he explained, was simply to protect the other members of the tribe, the bird discovering the snake would make the "LOOK OUT! THERE'S A SNAKE" call and everyone would flee to safety. But no. They did just the opposite. They all ran over to get close to the snake.

They weren't trying to dislodge the snake. The snake was certainly not going to leave the safety of the bush. They weren't trying to attack the snake because that would be too dangerous.

And, he pointed out, look at their posture. The birds were leaning forward, putting themselves at risk. Their wings were drooped. If they wanted to ensure a quick getaway, their wings would be raised above their bodies.

"So why are they doing this?" he asked us. Without waiting for an answer, he offered one.

"They are showing off. They are like children in the playground taunting a bully, showing how brave they are."

Why Birds Don't Just Tell You to Pish Off

That example and explanation made an impression on me, and, frankly, it makes a great deal of sense. It also brought me to give the matter of mobbing considerable thought, and I think now that birds engage in mobbing behavior at least in part because it's a break in the routine and livens up the day.

No, I'm not kidding. Put yourself in the place of a bird. Except when birds are nesting—busy engaging mates, defending territories, feeding and defending young—they have pretty boring lives. All they have to do over the course of the day is forage (usually relegated to the morning and evening hours), tend to a little toiletry, and try not to get eaten (which for most birds means staying quiet, still, and under cover).

There is a lot of time when birds are doing nothing, and it must be pretty tedious.

Then somebody starts raising a ruckus. You, the bird, don't know what's going on. It might be something important, and not knowing what it is might even be risky. So you go over to have a look. Maybe even get in on the action. Test your reflexes. See whether you've still got the right stuff.

And is this really any different than some of the behavior our species exhibits? You hear your neighbors having a really colorful domestic argument in their front yard. Don't you go over to the window, peek around the curtain, see what the hubbub is all about? You could be sitting in your La-Z-Boy studying the back of your eyelids, but it's more interesting watching the neighbors going at it.

Say you're sitting in a diner. You hear a loud crash and see a bunch of people surveying the remains of a piano embedded in the sidewalk. Don't you and all the other patrons walk over to get a firsthand damage assessment? Maybe offer some after-the-fact advice regarding the proper use of a block and tackle?

I'm not suggesting that you frequent the kinds of establishments where brawls are a common form of entertainment, but you've certainly seen such scenes enacted on the silver screen or late-night television (or don't you watch old John Wayne movies?). When the Duke is forced to defend dignity and honor by beating the tar out of some beefy and well-connected lout do all the other bar patrons just order another daiquiri or cosmopolitan and go back to discussing *The New York Times* best-seller list? No. They get up. Form a ring around the brawling pair. Lean forward. Scream encouragement. Throw a few uppercuts and right crosses into the air.

Why should birds be any different?

Several years ago, in late August, I saw a family group of Blue Jays engage in a mobbing action in front of a tree cavity that, at least in past years, had housed roosting Eastern Screech-Owls. One bird initiated the action. Flew to the tree. Took a perch near the opening. Fixed its eye on the hole and started screaming blue murder.

The other members of the tribe flew in, took perches, and added their voices to the ruckus. For several minutes they crowded around the hole, screaming invectives, raising holy hell. Several individuals even put their heads right into the cavity. Then, as suddenly as they began, the birds stopped. They stood around preening for a bit. Made assorted low, murmuring jay noises. Flew off, looking for . . . other diversions?

Curious, I climbed the tree and looked in. The cavity was empty.

If you like, you can conclude that jays are just stupid. Me? I think that jays are very intelligent and I think that these particular jays knew perfectly well that the cavity was empty. I think they were playing.

And I think birds respond to pishing in no small part because they are bored and curious. They engage in mobbing because being part of the action is more fun than sitting in the shadows, trying not to get eaten.

2 | The Elements of Pishing

There are as many styles of pishing as there are birders who pish. No two birders sound alike. No one sound or even combination of sounds is universal, surefire, works everywhere, every time, on every bird.

In fact, there are a number of times when pishing seems to have no effect on birds at all. We'll explore that later.

But over the years I've developed a style and sequence that seem to work often enough and widely enough for me to feel comfortable offering them to you. Feel free to experiment and tailor your repertoire to the birds of your region. And no matter what I say, remember that the real experts are not the birders imitating the sounds but the birds who coin them. Listen to the scolding calls of birds in your regions. Imitate *them*.

The Basic Pish

The most simple, basic, universal, and easily mimicked pish is the *psssh, psssh, psssh* call that resembles the scold of Tufted Titmouse and assorted other titmouse and chickadee species. If you've never heard a scolding tit, this description isn't going to be much use to you. It is somewhat akin to the hissing whispered *psssh* sound Aunt Mabel makes to gain the attention of her focus-challenged cat, but louder, more forceful, higher pitched, given with a rising inflection at the end and in a sequence of three that is repeated two or three times.

PussshEE, PussshEE, PussshEE; PussshEE, PussshEE, PussshEE.

Why three? I don't know. Maybe titmice can't count past three. Is it truly important to do it in sets of three? Probably not. I'm just going by what the experts do; scolding titmice usually vocalize in sets of three.

But whereas Aunt Mabel is trying to gain the attention of her somewhat oblivious cat, you are trying to incite a riot. Enunciated properly, your *PussshEE* should be somewhat shrill, whistled, and breathy, but strident. You've got to sound excited. You've got to sound *pished!* If your pish succeeds in getting the cat to walk up, wrap itself around your ankle, and purr, you're doing it wrong. If you can get the cat to raise its head, stare with eyes the size of saucers, and then run like hell in the other direction, you're doing it about right.

I once knew an ornithologist named Harold Axtell, a man who was to birding what Hammurabi was to law. He told me that when he pished he actually tried to imagine himself as a near apoplectic titmouse watching a rat snake inching toward his nest hole.

The sound is easy to make. Position your mouth as if to say *push.* Say it, but don't bite it off; let the air continue to whistle through your teeth and puckered lips. It's a *psssh, psssh, psssh* with the volume and force of a desperately venting steam valve. Now add a rising inflection at the end. *PussshEE!*

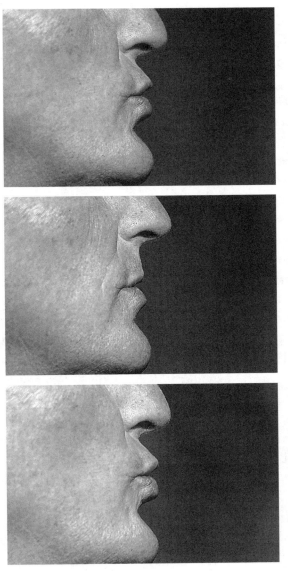

*The basic pish: lips puckered to pish, pause,
lips puckered to pish.*

If you have a whistle-enhancing gap between your front teeth, you are a born pisher. If Arnold Schwarzenegger ever takes up birding, he'll be a natural.

Variations on the Basic Pish

PussshEE, PussshEE, PussshEE is as basic as it gets. The Oh, Dick. Oh, Jane. Oh, Sally. Oh, see funny, funny Spot level of pishing. You can enhance the sense of urgency and vehemence by varying the rhythm and pattern—dragging on some notes and becoming more abrupt or emphatic on others.

Example: *PusssssshEE, PushE, PushE; PusssssshEEEE PushE/PushE . . .*

Larding a stutter into the sequence seems to raise the bar on bird response. The stutter is a simple *Pss* (the sound you would make if you were trying to surreptitiously gain someone's attention under somewhat circumspect circumstances) but doubled. For example: *Pss/Pss* or *P'Pss*. Tucked into a pish sequence, it might fall like this:

PusssssshEE, PusshE, PusshE; P'Pss PusssssshEE PusshE, PusshE; P'Pss . . .

So not only do you sound pished, you are stuttering pished.

Again and always, listen to the professionals, to the real scolding birds. It's their pattern you are trying to emulate, not mine.

Something Upon Which to Vent Their Spleen

The purpose of the basic pish is to alert all within hearing distance that there is something rotten in bird-dom. You don't have to worry about being ignored. Evolution has pretty much weeded out inattentiveness in birds. You do have to worry about holding their attention (birds have short attention spans) and about getting them to take the next step, which is to come over and see what the problem is.

It helps to give birds, if not an actual body to kick, then at least a phantom soul to damn. Try imitating the call of an avian predator such as an owl or a hawk.

You can try imitating a rat snake but the sound won't travel very far.

My stand-in villain of choice is the Eastern Screech-Owl—a very common, mostly nocturnal predator whose daytime presence drives small birds into a vengeful frenzy and whose call, once learned, is both easy to imitate and easy on your vocal apparatus. Despite the species' limited range—across the eastern United States and southern Canada west to the Great Plains—the call works well in western North America too (Western Screech-Owl vocalizations are not that different and, in fact, Western Screech-Owl will respond to the call of Eastern). I have also used it to good effect in Africa and South America.

How come? I don't know. Maybe it's atavistic. Maybe the calls of Eastern Screech-Owl approximate the sounds that small bird-eating dinosaurs used when ordering off the menu.

Eastern Screech-Owls have two calls that can be used alternately. The first is a low, even, quavering warble (lasting three to five seconds). The second is a rising and falling horselike whinny (lasting one to two seconds). The first call is the bird's more commonly uttered song. The whinny is used to drive intruding birds (meaning other screech-owls) out of the area. It sounds angry, and it is.

TRACK
2

Point of departure. In order to mimic this call, you must be able to whistle. If this celebrated bit of vocal artistry is beyond your capacity, skip the rest of this section. Go directly to "Squeal."

But if you can whistle, start with a low-pitched, even whistle—the lower pitched the better. If you have a pitch pipe (or, even better, perfect pitch), somewhere around A flat is about right.

Now comes the tricky part.

You need to form a gob of spit and position it, comfortably, somewhere between the middle and back of your tongue. Then elevate your chin slightly and whistle through the spit. The spit, by dint of a mini wave action, breaks up the whistle, causing it to quaver. The force of the whistle keeps the spit seated on your tongue and prevents it from trickling down your throat.

If you start to sputter or choke, your head is too far back. Drop your chin.

If saliva starts trickling out of the corners of your mouth, raise your chin.

That's right. Like so much of life, you have to strike a balance—in this case between the angle of your chin and the force of your whistle. To see what works for you, try forming a bolus of spit, centering it on your tongue, and whistling with your chin level. This will cause you to whistle over, not through, the spit producing a whistle that is even and unbroken. Slowly elevate your chin. The spit and the flow of the air should engage, causing the whistle to quaver.

By the way, if you have a cold or chronic sinus condition, so much the better. Viscous spit beats weak spit. It's easier to manipulate and gives you a slower and more controlled wave action.

If you listen closely to the call of a real Eastern Screech-Owl you will note that the warble is usually not truly even. It starts soft and slow gaining volume with a more accelerated warble at the end. Note, too, that the end is abrupt.

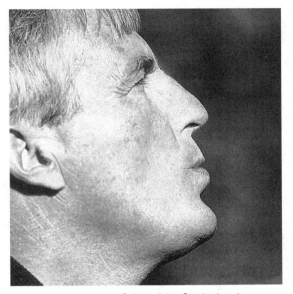

The proper angle of the chin for imitating an Eastern Screech-Owl. Chin higher, you sputter and choke. Chin lower, you have saliva trickling out of the corner of your mouth.

The whinny call is more difficult to reproduce but is done in much the same fashion as the warble. Instead of a low, even whistle, the whistle rises and falls—somewhat like an exaggerated whistle expressing appreciative surprise. In the movies this whistle is usually followed by the expression "Golly" or "Gee willikers."

The initial rising part of the whinny is mostly clear (no warble). The warble kicks in on the descent. Many people can imitate the whinny without resorting to spit, letting the diaphragm control the whistle and impart the quaver.

I know, I know. Stop. You're right. Some people simply cannot manipulate their whistle or their spit to make this sound. But before you conclude that it is impossible, you should know that my younger brother Dave was able to accomplish this feat while he was still in the crib. And he didn't even have the motivation of being a birder.

A Little Toot Will Do Ya

Eastern Screech-Owl is by no means the only small bird-eating owl in North America (it's not even the only screech-owl). In many places, birds will react just as well or even better to the calls of indigenous species—the birding equivalent of a fly fisherman "matching the hatch" (i.e., seeing what insects the trout are feeding on today and finding a fly pattern that resembles them).

Across much of the West—from the western prairies to the Pacific North, through western British Columbia to extreme southeastern Alaska and south into Mexico)—Western Screech-Owl is the common bird-eating predator, and its call is easily imitated. The call consists of a series of five to ten low, mellow, hooted whistles that starts slow and gains tempo at the end (with the last notes running together somewhat). It's as if the Eastern Screech-Owl whinny were played at a lower, slower speed represented by points (hoots) connected with a line. This species also utters a two-part trill—a short trill followed by a longer one.

The Whiskered Screech-Owl, a Mexican and Central American species whose range just reaches southeastern Arizona and southwestern New Mexico, also hoots. The typical song consists of about eight short, low, evenly spaced hoots that fall off or drop in pitch at the end. This species also makes a halting, broken pattern of hoots that recalls the dots-and-dashes pattern of Morse code.

But across much of the west, the owl that birds love to hate is the diminutive Northern Pygmy-Owl, a long-tailed, Hermit Thrush-sized, daytime hunter. The sight of this species drives small songbirds into a frenzy. Its simple and easily imitated call incites western birds as quickly as the warble of Eastern Screech-Owl incites eastern species—in fact, it works well in the East too, very probably because in quality and pattern it is similar to the song of Northern Saw-whet Owl (another bird-eating villain in the eyes of songbirds).

Northern Pygmy-Owl's song consists of a series of fairly slow, mellow, even, well-spaced single- or double-note toots that goes on and on: *too. too. too. too. too. too . . .* or *too-too. too-too. too-too. too-too . . .* The tempo is variable. Pauses between notes may be short or fairly lengthy.

By comparison, the toot of Northern Saw-whet Owl has the same mellow tonal qualities, but the delivery is often quicker, and the notes are, strictly speaking, not so evenly paced. The delivery sounds tired, as though the bird were bored or perhaps trying to catch its breath in places, causing slight breaks in the rhythm.

In actual fact, I'm not sure that the details really make any difference. Any series of low, even, continuous, tooting whistles seems to incite a reaction from small to medium-sized woodland songbirds.

Other Villains?

Where Barred Owls occur, their calls are to mobbing action what a detonator is to an explosion. Forest birds respond readily to the owl's classic *Who cooks for you. Who cooks for YOU-all* call, but for some reason, the call of this species seems to really irk birds living in Canadian-zone woodlands.

I remember on one occasion leading a field trip in Maine and trying my pishing prowess on a group of Black-capped Chickadees (one of the planet's most pish-prone species). My very well-executed rendition of Eastern Screech-Owl, a song that has gotten me repeated encores from chickadees from Massachusetts to Texas, didn't even garner a yawn from these Down East black-caps.

Then it hit me. I was north of the range of Eastern Screech-Owl, and chickadees are, for the most part, nonmigratory. So I tried imitating Barred Owl (which breeds north to the Maritimes and across southern Quebec). And although my Barred Owl is, I am forced to admit, not even good enough to get me on the amateur hour, in about 0.00239 second five very pished-off chickadees shed their laconic reserve and got right in my face, demanding to know what was the great, big, hairy *dee, dee, deal.*

I have also had some minor success attracting birds by imitating the high, thin, down-slurred whistle of Red-tailed Hawks (*s/wEEEerrr*). And when trying to locate nesting Cooper's Hawks by imitating their "cacking" call, the occasional songbird has responded.

But if birding were golf and I were limited in my repertoire of calls as golfers are limited in the number of clubs they can carry, then I would limit myself to three calls: The Eastern Screech-Owl warble. The Northern Saw-whet and Northern Pygmy-Owl toot. The Barred Owl "Who cooks for you."

"Wait a minute," you're saying, "that's four, not three."

Oh well. I'd probably cheat at golf, too.

Use Everything, Including the Squeal

Let's summarize. You've uttered your basic pish, putting birds on alert. You've let them know that one of those heinous, bird-murdering owls had the unforgivable temerity to flout all articles of decent behavior and live on the face of this earth.

And it's daylight (the bird is thinking). And I've got the advantage (it's thinking). And right and might are on my side. And there isn't anything else clogging the docket at the moment. Besides, I'm bored. And . . .

Usually, this is enough to incite a mobbing action. You can keep alternating pish sequences with owl calls until new birds stop coming in, until you've seen enough, or until the birds you've incited get bored and leave (the most likely possibility).

But sometimes even a well-executed pish and a convincingly proffered villain are not enough to incite a mobbing reaction. In places where birds are frequently subjected to pishing or in situations where birds are distant (such as the very tops of trees in a mature forest), *sometimes* you need a little added stimulus.

So you up the ante. Increase the drama. Introduce an element of murder and mayhem.

Going back to the example of the piano committing osculation with the sidewalk: If it was just a piano and a sidewalk, you'd walk over to investigate. But if the piano fell on a passerby who was crying for help, you'd most likely run.

My Surefire, Patent-Pending, Reluctant-Bird-Reforming Squeal Call

It was fall, migratory prime time. I was overlooking a plowed field near the Cape May Point Lighthouse. There were a few birds about—starlings, pipits, and Killdeer in the field, with assorted woodland species foraging along the edge. I was watching a pretty impressive late-season hawk flight and even saw a young Cooper's Hawk fold up and dive like a vengeful missile.

One of the feeding starlings did not—at least not in time.

The hawk caught the starling in flight and, instead of heading for the safety of the trees, lit upon the ground. The starling, trapped in the hawk's talons but otherwise, apparently, uninjured, began to scream.

SkreEEEuh, SkreEEEuh, SkreEEEuh, SkreEEEuh . . .

It was loud and shrill, defiant but heartrending. It made the hair on the back of my neck stand up and my ears beg for the mercy of silence. It . . .

Prompted every bird within earshot to fly to the entwined duo, adding their cries and harassing actions to the unfolding drama. Some landed and called. Some hovered overhead. Some dove at the hawk, making it duck.

Recognizing its strategic disadvantage, the hawk lifted off (carrying the screaming starling with it) and disappeared into the woods with the avian posse hot on its rectacies.

No, I don't know how the story ended. I only know that I had never seen so many birds respond so quickly to another bird's cries.

It took me only about two minutes to figure out how to imitate it.

> "I make an old lady blush. I make a young girl squeal."
>
> —George Thorogood, "Bad to the Bone"

If you can kiss, you can squeal. Wet your lips with your tongue. Form a closed-mouth pucker, keeping your lips pressed tightly, repeat *tightly,* together. Suck in. The result should be a high, thin, slightly squeaky, squealing sound lasting perhaps half a second. Done properly, it should recall the sound of mice—in fact, in might help if you consciously try and imitate the squeak of a mouse.

But well done or not, the sound is not very loud, not very shrill, not easy to execute, and not very convincing—certainly not convincing enough to get every bird within earshot to come to your aid. I realize this. The purpose of the exercise was to demonstrate that the source of the squeal sound is your lips.

Now try this: Press your index and middle fingers against your freshly licked, pursed, and compressed lips (palm facing you). Kiss—just the way you did before. The sound should be louder and higher pitched.

The pressure of your fingers on your lips makes a tighter seal, allowing you to squeal at a higher pitch. Also, the narrow gully between your fingers (and perhaps your cupped hand) serves as a resonating chamber, amplifying the sound (just as the body of a guitar amplifies the sound of a plucked string).

You can test this. Try squealing with your slightly parted fingers pressed against your lips. Then do it with your fingers pressed together.

SkreEEEuh, SkreEEEuh, SkreEEEuh . . . Do it ten to twenty times.

What you should be getting is a slightly rising and falling squeal with mouselike squeakiness and the soothing properties of a dentist's drill. Done properly, people will find it painful to stand near you (yes, it's that piercing).

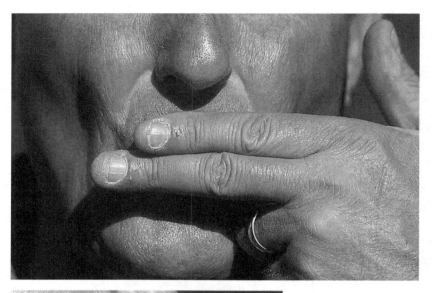

The proper hand position for both the squeal and the chip: two fingers, tight compression on the lips. Kiss! Note the concave cheeks, but don't suck so hard you pull the fillings out of your teeth.

If you are not getting the desired effect (if your squeal sounds more like the call of a dispirited Wood Frog than an angry mouse), don't suck harder; it's more likely that your lips are not pressed together tightly enough.

You don't have to give yourself a hernia to make this sound. If you start pulling fillings out of your teeth, stop. Like the screech-owl warble, it's a matter of finding the right balance and getting the elements to work in concert. When you figure it out, making the squeal call is only slightly more effortful than kissing.

And how hard is that?

As Easy as Pish, Warble, Squeal

That's it. The boiler-plate sequence: Pish, warble, squeal. In general, it is best to lead off with either the pish or the screech-owl warble. Depending on whim, the situation, or my understanding of the particular species that I'm trying to attract, I do both. Don't be too quick to employ the squeal call. And the first time you introduce it into the pish sequence, don't dwell on it for long. An initial series of ten squeals followed immediately with a hearty round of basic pish sounds is plenty.

The squeal says, "Somebody is in a real world of hurt over here," and birds, endowed with a strong sense of self-preservation, might conclude, "Case closed, better him than me," and head the other way. In fact, often when the squeal call is used first, or alone, birds respond precisely that way.

Backing up the squeal call with some basic pishes assures other birds that, at the very least, they won't be facing the unknown alone.

The response time of birds varies. At times, birds come in quickly (sometimes immediately). At other times birds must be coaxed. And again, at other times, there is no response at all. There may be no birds around, no species that are easily pish-piqued, or just too many things working against you to get a response—these include weather, time of day, time of year, the physical condition of the birds, and whether you are the first or the fiftieth person to test their pishability that day. Using conditions to your best advantage will be discussed later. For now . . .

Unless I'm confident that birds are present, or unless there is a particular species that I am driven to see, I commonly stop pishing after one or, at most, two minutes if no response or a limited response is forthcoming.

Any Other Calls?

Certainly. There are lots of species and lots of scold calls—unfortunately, many of them are not easily imitated (at least not by me). But there are four that can be very useful: The chip, the sequential chip, the whisper pish and the knockdown pish.

The most common and widespread vocalization emanating from the mouths of songbirds is very arguably the chip. You would have to be a fairly exceptional birder to note and appreciate the many subtle inflections that different species impart to this simple utterance. Mercifully, for the purposes of gaining the attention of birds, you need to know none of this.

All you need to know is how to make a good, loud, sharp, no-nonsense chip. Let the birds try to figure out whether it's being made by a Black Phoebe, American Redstart, or Lark Sparrow.

Birds most commonly chip when they are excited, anxious, or agitated. Like a scolding vocalization, it tells other birds that something is happening in the neighborhood that is worthy of their attention—maybe even their investigation.

When I was a young birder I was told that the best way to produce this sound was to "kiss the back of your thumb." Know what? It works. Press your lips to the back of your thumb. Give it a high, sharp, squeaky kiss.

Do you actually need the back of your thumb? No. Just like the squeal call, the sound is made with the lips. The back of your thumb just makes it easier to compress your lips.

But like the squeal call, I find that I can get a louder, sharper, fuller-bodied, and more convincing chip by bringing my index and middle fingers up to my lips (as if I were going to make the squeal call) but treat them to a kissing chip instead of a prolonged sucking squeal.

Kiss my thumb, and I've got a high, sharp chip that sounds Yellow Warbler sharp. Kiss the inside of my fingers, and I've got a rich, robust, full-bodied CHIP that would instill envy in an Ovenbird (or maybe even a Northern Waterthrush).

Playing for Sparrows: Marshaling Your Chips

The bad news about making a chip note is that it's really hard on the jaw muscles. It's not the kind of call you want to string into a lengthy sequence (although, in some cases, this can be very effective). The good news is that often a single chip or two is all it takes.

This is (mirabile dictu) often the case with sparrows. If you are unfamiliar with this tribe of feathered miscreants, sparrows are relatively shy and cryptically garbed birds that spend much of their time on or near the ground and amuse themselves by hiding from and frustrating the aspirations of birders. Many sparrow species seem wholly or partially immune to most forms of pishing. You are often first alerted to the presence of a sparrow when it takes off, usually at close quarters, and then disappears into the grass or brush some distance away.

Some sparrow species, those that forage in flocks particularly in winter, often fly only a short distance from the flush point, and burrow into the closest woody edge or protective cover. Try this: Wait a decent interval—thirty seconds or so. Give the birds a chance to calm down. Then bring your fingers up and make a single, sharp *chip!* If this doesn't work, try another or a double chip. *Chip! Chip!*

Often, just a single exclamatory chip will prompt one or more birds to jump to an open perch as if to exclaim "What? Where? Who did that?" before burrowing themselves, once again, in the thick stuff. Be ready. Have your binoculars in hand and prefocused to that spot. Your look may be brief, and once they've been gulled, sparrows are often loath to make a repeat appearance.

Nonflocking, mostly grassland species (such as Grasshopper and Le Conte's Sparrows) are very difficult to coax into the open but can, at times, be enticed to poke their heads above their grassy fortress. If you flush a single grassland sparrow, quickly note where the bird launched itself and calculate the distance from yourself. That's the bird's approximate flush distance. You can approach somewhere short of that point. Now note where the bird lands. Walk toward that point, stopping short of the established flush distance (in fact, give yourself a buffer because the bird is now nervous and alert). Wait. Try a chip or two—or eight or nine.

I'm not going to lie to you. For these species, success is limited.

Something that often does work for a variety of sparrows (and other open-country, grassland, marshland, and desert species) is the squeal call. More on this later.

Rebooting the Mobbing Action: It Takes a Stack of Chips

As mentioned, birds have short attention spans. Even when you succeed in inciting a mobbing action, birds soon realize that the loudly touted disruption to their peace and security boils down to you, and, frankly, you aren't worth bothering further with.

You can often reboot the mobbing reaction by injecting a series of chips into your standard pish sequence—the louder and sharper the better: *Chip . . . chip . . . chip . . . chip . . . chip . . .*

Birds that are beginning to get bored and drift away become reactivated and vocal again. Birds that have left the area often return. It might be that the sudden eruption of chips is interpreted by other birds to mean: "Well, maybe *I* don't see anything to get all worked up about, but that new guy over there sure sounds yanked. Maybe I missed something."

I got the idea by observing the reaction of mobbing birds to Ovenbirds—chunky, olive-brown, bead-breasted, ground-loving warblers of eastern forests. Ovenbirds are often among the last birds to respond to a mobbing action, but once they arrive (much like guests who arrive late to a party) it is almost impossible to get them to leave.

Time and time again I noticed that the loud, incessant *tChep . . . tChep . . . tChep . . . tChep . . .* call of an Ovenbird brought new life to the party (and the chip note I try to imitate when making the sequential chip belongs to Ovenbird).

In full pish mode, proving that one can pish and scan at the same time.

Word of caution. The sequential chip is a technique of last resort. It is really hard on the jaw muscles, and you won't be able to keep it up for long.

Shhhhh. When Shouting Fails, Try Whispering

The manly art of pishing, as it is widely practiced, calls for birders to throw as much volume and vehemence as they can into their pishes. When several ardent pishers band together, a form of mass "pishteria" often takes hold. One pisher tries to outpish the next, and if no birds appear, the stakes get higher and the vehemence and the volume increase.

If you go to a very popular birding area on a slow day it is not uncommon to see half a dozen bull pishers all standing around auspicious bushes or strategic stretches of trail sounding like a chorus of perforated steam pipes. They maintain this performance until the biggest, baddest, most tenacious pisher among them wheezes to a stop—by tacit agreement and default certifying that the area is 110-percent bird free, supporting what they already knew (that it was a slow birding day). Then the group moves on to the next spot.

But are places subjected to saturation pishing really bird free?

I once knew a shy, demure young birder named Claire who often brought her considerable skills to bear on certifiably bird-free zones. Her secret? While other birders shouted, Claire whispered.

After waiting for the pishing bulls to leave, granting time for tranquility to sooth the pish-ravaged landscape, Claire would step quietly off the trail. Sit. Start making soft, soothing, barely audible pishing noises.

psssh . . . psssh . . . pssssh . . . [long pause] *. . . psssh . . . psssh . . . pssssh . . .* [long pause]

She would do this for two . . . five . . . up to ten minutes and . . .

Low and behold, slowly, furtively, birds would begin to edge forward. A Gray Catbird here, a Yellow Warbler there, maybe a Northern Waterthrush or a skulkiferous, tangle-loving Worm-eating Warbler. The birds weren't agitated or spoiling for a fight (as they commonly are when pish-piqued). Often as not they would not even signal their presence or approach by calling (until sighting Claire). They were approaching because *they were curious.*

And if their curiosity was aroused only by a desire to understand what would prompt a birder to spend so much time sitting in a tick-infested woodland, what difference does it make?

"Victory," as some deep-thinking military philosopher once observed, "is a means of pragmatic verification." For whatever reason, Claire would attract reticent birds by invoking the power of the whisper pish when other measures failed.

Being one of the pishing bulls, I've never had enough patience to exploit this technique—but I recognize and respect success. During pishing workshops or seminars, I often extoll the virtues of the whisper pish and encourage birders to try it.

A couple of years ago, I got a letter from a birder in Arizona who, while engaged in a Christmas Bird Count, heard a call note emanating from a brushy hillside that she couldn't place. Going through her entire pish repertoire several times and failing to get a response, she suddenly remembered my lecture and my reference to Claire and the whisper pish. Having nothing to lose, she tried it.

And succeeded in drawing out a Rufous-capped Warbler for the count—something that no bull pisher has ever accomplished north of the Mexican border.

The Knockdown Pish

Here's a scenario that is all too common: You're standing in the open, near some bushes, trees, or a wooded edge. A bird flies by, moving too quickly to bring your binoculars to bear (and chances are that you couldn't identify it unless it was stationary anyway). What do you do? Shrug? Swallow your disappointment?

Try getting the bird to land. Try making a knockdown pish.

It's easy to do (only the discipline to use it is hard to instill because too often you remember to give this technique a try only after the bird is gone).

But the next time some reasonably close, fast-flying song-bird goes hurling by, go: *PSHEW!* or *PSHEW!/PSHEW!*

Often the bird will head for the nearest cover and take a perch, giving you the opportunity you need.

The knockdown pish is a loud, breathy, explosive, sharply truncated pish. You form the sound much the same way you make the basic pish sound—except that the force of the sound is visceral. You bring the force of your diaphragm into play, letting air explode through your lips and your teeth. It's a rocket-propelled pish.

PSHEW!

It sounds a little bit like a loud, breathy White-throated Sparrow alarm call, but what I aspire to, what I consciously try to imitate when making this sound, is the explosive call note of Evening Grosbeak.

Why does it prompt birds to land? Because the bird is in the open. Somebody just shouted an alarm. *PSHEW!* Look out! Danger! Without better intelligence, few birds want to risk being the only obvious target in the sky (the warning could, after all, relate to the presence of a falcon). So the bird grabs the nearest perch to size up the situation.

Be ready when you pish. Based on the bird's trajectory and desire to get out of the air fast, you can often guess where it's going to land. Your look might be brief (if the bird chooses to dive for cover) or more lengthy if the bird sees nothing amiss.

And if the bird keeps going? Yes, they often do that. But most of the time, at the very least, you'll get the bird to veer sharply or contemplate taking a perch (giving you some small measure of empowerment over the birds of the air).

Besides, the bird was just going to fly by anyway. What did you have to lose?

Word of warning: With so much *oomph* behind this call, it's not uncommon to project more than sound. When birding with others, make sure that your lips are pointed in a safe direction to avoid collateral damage and embarrassing apologies. And never use this technique with food in your mouth.

Pish Perfect, or Every Good Bird Deserves Pish

It is possible that there are people who are born to pish (which is different from being a born pisher). My brother Dave, remember, mastered the screech-owl warble while still in the crib. But even the most genetically endowed pishophiles reach proficiency only through practice.

The best way to practice is to go birding. Try the basic sounds. Tailor them to your vocal abilities and to your audience.

What audience? The birds, silly. Watch the birds. It's the whole point of this exercise. But don't watch them just for gratification. Watch them to see how they are (or, as importantly, are not) reacting to your vocal tweaking.

If you hit a sound or sequence that gets a species' hackles up, file it away. Put it in your repertoire. If you're throwing everything at them but the audio kitchen sink, try changing pitch, changing the sequence, or . . .

Just walk away. Some birds are a tough audience. Find one that's going to be more attentive and forgiving. When you are first putting together your pish, positive feedback is very important.

It's important to listen to birds too. They are after all the professionals. Their scolding sounds constitute the efforts of true born pishers. It's how I learned to interject a descending stutter call into my basic pish sequence. Several vireo species (Yellow-throated, Blue-headed, Plumbeous, and Cassin's) all make an admonishing *Ch'Chih'chu'chu'chu* when agitated. It sounds as if the birds are imitating the sound of an old steam locomotive (a.k.a. choo-choo) at full throttle, but each raspy, breathy puff in the sequence drops in pitch.

Throwing this call into the pish sequence after a minute or two of hearty pishing has two advantages. First, it suggests to other birds that a new ally has joined the fray (lending credence and support). Second, it's an easy call to imitate and execute. After a couple of minutes of pishing, your jaws might need a rest, and this call is almost like a balm for tired jaw muscles.

There is, of course, nothing to stop you from practicing your pish at home or on the way to work. But insofar as pishing is a somewhat arcane art, you might want to save yourself the trouble of unnecessary explanations (which probably won't be believed anyway) and time your hours of practice to fall within hours of solitude.

If, for example, you are polishing your squeal call in front of the cat and your teenage daughter comes in with the newest, greatest, potentially ultimate love of her life, there might be a great deal of social ground to make up (on her part and yours).

If, as another example, you conclude that the subway at rush hour would make a great place to practice your basic pish, there is a high probability that some Good Samaritan will mistakenly conclude that you have aspirated a breath mint and subject you to a diaphragm-rupturing Heimlich maneuver (thus crippling your hopes of ever mastering the knockdown pish).

If you fall into that broad band of the human spectrum that commutes to work alone in your car, you will soon discover that those hours behind the wheel constitute an ideal place to practice your pish.

Several words of warning: First, make sure that you have a stock of tissues or paper towels on hand to be used to wipe down the inside of your windshield and clean your rearview mirror between bouts of enthusiastic pishing.

Also, if sitting in traffic, be careful not to catch the eye of the person behind you while practicing a full-pucker pish (the gesture might be misconstrued). Also, be mindful of open windows.

Many years ago, I was sitting at an intersection in my VW bug, waiting for an unusually long light to change. I'd just gotten the hang of making the screech-owl warble (I'm not as gifted as my brother Dave in this regard) and was practicing with, as it turned out, a false sense of security.

It was late February but unusually warm—near 70! Like so many other drivers that day I'd rolled down the windows in my car to enjoy the first springlike temperatures of the year. One of those other drivers was the woman stopped next to me, whose expression of horrified fascination remained fixed even after the light changed and I made my getaway.

Ma'am, in case you're reading this, I'm really sorry, and I hope I didn't startle you.

3 | Making Your Pishes Count

arold Axtell once observed that "pishing will do one of three things. Either it will attract birds, scare them away, or do nothing."

Which of these three behavior patterns will manifest itself depends on many things—not a few of which are within a birder's control. There is more to being an accomplished pisher than effectively and convincingly imitating bird sounds.

What All the Beautiful Pishers Are Wearing

Birds are sensitive to color, and they are particularly mindful of bright colors. When birding, particularly in woodlands or open, monotone habitats (such as marshes or grasslands), you will have greater success getting close to birds if you avoid bright, light colors. In particular avoid wearing white. It is nature's universal signal for "DANGER" and says, "Look out. If you value your life, stay away from here."

But, you are thinking, if you are trying to incite a mobbing action, wouldn't it be to your advantage to advertise, "Hey, look. The risk is over here."?

No. Don't forget, a mobbing action is a means, not an end. What you are trying to do is get birds to leave their protective cover and approach close enough so that you can see and study them. If you are standing on a dark woodland trail and you are wearing a bright white T-shirt (size XL) bearing the boast "5th Annual Condor Watch and Tequila Bust," you're going to stand out like a flare on a moonless night. An approaching bird will be able to see you just fine from behind a latticework of leaves and branches and may find very little reason to get any closer.

If, on the other hand, you were dressed in dark greens or browns, you'd be harder to see, possibly less threatening, and birds will likely feel comfortable approaching closer or, better still, be obliged to get closer to see who and what you are.

Are there any hard data supporting the supposition that white scares birds away? I know of none. What I do know is that many professional tour leaders discourage group members from wearing white. Also, as a longtime hunter, I know, from many hours spent sitting in tree-stands in full camo that birds are indifferent, bordering upon curious, when I am so cryptically garbed. On those occasions when I have been motivated to pish while hunting, I have had birds approach to within inches of my face and more than once, birds have landed on me.

I'm not saying that you need to replace your arsenal of birding T-shirts with a wardrobe of camo patterns like Mossy Oak Break-Up, Advantage, and Extra Gray Realtree (but for the record, I think Mossy Oak Break-Up makes wearers melt into woodlands and that Extra Gray Realtree is a wonderful all-around open-country and woodland camo pattern). I'm just saying that if you want to go birding and you like bright colors, please don't bird near me.

By the way, did I mention that you'll also want clothing that is quiet? When pishing, often your first clue that a bird is approaching comes from hearing its call. If you have a choice between fleece and Gore-Tex, go with fleece.

Finding a Plot to Pish In

If *psssh, psssh, psssh* were a magic incantation, practitioners could stand anywhere and birds would appear. Well, it's not magic. It's just a technique linked to the same cause-and-effect relationships that bind the other elements of the universe— that's the bad news. The good news is that if you are intelligent with respect to how, where, and when you apply your cause, the effects will be more satisfying.

This is just a complicated way of saying that you are better off pishing in some places than in others.

Pishing on the Edge

One of the most common mistakes incipient pishers make is standing out in the open, too far from cover. Yes, I know that trails through birding areas are often set back from the forest edge, but to be effective, if you plan to pish, you should be right up against the woodlands (five to ten feet). Why so close? Three reasons.

First, if you are standing out in the middle of a field adjacent to woodlands or in a large clearing in the middle of a forest, no forest bird is going to approach. Forest birds are perching birds, and they need someplace to land.

Second, by standing away from the vegetation, your eyes will be fixed on its outer layer. You will not be able to peer back into the forest itself. Even birds attracted to your pishing are

Wrong. *Woodland birds are, by and large, perching birds, and perching birds are not going to fly into an open area devoid of perches no matter how good a pisher you are.*

likely to halt before reaching the outer limits of the vegetation and study the situation from partial concealment. You'll never see them.

Third, the closer you are to a bird, the more likely it is to respond. The farther away you are, the easier it is for the birds to blow you off. If your objective is to entice woodland birds into the open, get close to or even into the woodlands.

Most pishers prefer to stand. It gives you mobility. It often keeps you above low, dense vegetation that may block your view. But there are some situations in which it is better to sit—

Right. Up against
the wooded edge—a
great plot to pish in.

in places where you have an open view or when a target species (e.g., Connecticut Warbler) hugs the ground. I know one very experienced birder who habitually crouches or kneels when he pishes. He insists that it presents a less intimidating profile and that birds respond more confidently.

The Perfect Pishable Place

If I were to design a pish-perfect habitat, it would be a small, wooded clearing (perhaps a widened portion of a dirt road) with a low, slightly broken canopy (about forty feet high), and a thick, complex understory with lots of intruding pockets (making it easier to peer deeper and increasing the amount of

In the New Jersey highlands—a mixed coniferous-deciduous forest and prime pishable habitat—during the summer of 1986.

surface area for birds to expose themselves). The place would have a wraparound quality, with low branches (ten to fifteen feet high) reaching overhead and to either side so that the birds have someplace to land in close proximity. The equally well-structured forest behind me should be less than forty feet away so birds would feel comfortable vaulting the open space to join the ruckus on the side you choose to watch.

What determines which side you choose to watch? If it is a factor, you want the sun behind you. In the early morning (particularly on a cool morning), you'll favor the side gathering the most sunlight (insect activity will be greater there). Later, in the heat of the day, you'll probably have more success with the cooler, shady side (particularly if it is warm).

You also want relative silence. You want near-windless conditions. You want companions who know how to keep still and keep their feet out of the gravel on the side of the road.

Most of all, you want chickadees.

Will Stop for Titmice

Many people harbor a fundamental misconception with regard to pishing. They presume that the objective of pishing is to tweak and attract all the birds within earshot. This is not so. For pishing to be successful, all you need to do is send one or two easily pish-piqued species into a stuttering rage. Let them galvanize all the other birds in the forest.

Across North America, there is arguably no group of birds more easily piqued by pishing than the tits, a group of fifteen species that includes chickadees, titmice, Verdin, and Bushtit. Not all species are found everywhere. In fact, some, like the Bridled Titmouse, a bird of oak woodlands in the desert South-west, and Gray-headed Chickadee, an arctic species that in North America is found only in Alaska, have limited ranges. Nevertheless, there are few locations and few habitats enjoying even a measure of woody vegetation that do not host one or more tit species.

Strictly speaking, from a pisher's standpoint, the more tits, the merrier.

That's not all. Not only are tits easily tweaked, they are vocal, even chatty, so all year they quickly alert birders to their presence. It gets even better. Tits often join and form the foundation of feeding flocks in winter and during migration. Chances are, outside the breeding season, if you hear chickadees or titmice, other birds—nuthatches, some woodpeckers, kinglets, and (in more temperate regions) vireos and warblers—will be in close association. Feeding flocks play follow the leader. If you can draw in a few pish-piqued chickadees, the pack will follow.

Almost anywhere in North America, the best and most effective strategy there is for finding birds is to simply be alert for the sounds of chickadees and titmice and the sputtering nattering of bushtits. Position yourself so that you will be able to see birds easily and well. Start pishing. Get ready for action.

Other Pishable Habitats, Other Pishable Birds

As discussed early on in this book, pishing is a technique that works best for woodland or forest birds. It is somewhat less successful in other habitats but it is certainly not wholly ineffective in most (I'm hesitant to say all) habitats. In fact, its effect on species that are anything but woodland can sometimes surprise you.

Many sparrow species respond well to squealing and chips. Sparrows of woodland edges (Song, White-throated, White-crowned, Harris's, Fox, and Lincoln's, along with towhees and juncos) respond well to a variety of pishes. Other sparrows of more brushy, open, grassy (or marshy) areas (Savannah, Brewer's, Chipping, Clay-colored, American Tree, Swamp, Field, and Vesper) are also fairly to very responsive.

Pure grassland and desert sparrow species are somewhat less responsive, but some may at times (and most notably during the breeding season) respond to chips or squealing. Less pish resistant are the sharp-tailed sparrows (Nelson's and Saltmarsh) and Seaside Sparrow, which are all fairly responsive to the squeal call. Their initial response is to sit up on taller grass. If you are persistent (and your squeal is damn good), they may even approach (covering a distance of perhaps fifty yards).

It was actually while trying to squeak up Saltmarsh Sharp-tailed Sparrows that I discovered that pishing (more specifically, squealing) attracts shorebirds.

Pishable Peeps

It is my perennial misfortune that saltmarsh sparrows are always on the far side of a tidal creek, leaving me no other resort than trying to pish them up. On this occasion, I was on the south dike at Brigantine National Wildlife Refuge (just north of Atlantic City). It was August, shorebird prime time, and the tide was out. The tidal creek, standing between me and the sparrow-rich tidal marsh beyond, was an amalgam of Least Sandpipers and mud.

I didn't bother with a standard pish, since its effectiveness on saltmarsh sparrows is often marginal. Instead I started squealing—a high, plaintive keening so heartrending it would garner sympathy from a sphinx.

While my eyes were trained on the tall grass lining the far bank, I couldn't help but notice that my vocalization had prompted about a hundred Least Sandpipers to grow animated and agitated and then take flight. They gathered in a massed ball (as many flocking species do when attempting to evade a predator) and started to fly in a tight circle around me.

Then they landed on the road, almost at my feet.

I was so shocked that I stopped squealing. The birds stood looking up at me. I looked down at them. After about ten seconds the birds took off as a flock and returned to the creek.

Not quite able to believe what I had just seen, I tried it again, and it happened again. Subsequently I've learned that Semipalmated Sandpipers also exhibit a similar behavior and that Least Sandpipers can, individually, be coaxed to approach by squealing when they are breeding.

Why would a flock of shorebirds respond to squealing? I don't know. Unless it's the same motivation that drives other species.

Pishing for the Big Ones

Back when I used to participate in multiple Christmas Bird Counts, I noticed an interesting phenomenon. At the end of the day, as the count compilers were going through the checklist and they hit the raptors, they'd call out a species name, and if nobody answered in the affirmative (meaning nobody saw that species during the day), they'd look accusingly at me.

True, I have a reputation for being a "raptor man." Also true I had a pretty good track record when it came to garnering birds of prey on Christmas counts. Those compilers probably attributed my success to the many thousands of hours I'd spent watching hawks at Cape May, or perhaps to the fact that I'd coauthored a book treating hawk identification.

Not one, I am sure, guessed the secret of my success.

Which had little to do with my raptor-finding skills. The reason I found more hawks than most other participants was that I was a really good pisher.

Most of the Sharp-shinned and Cooper's Hawks that I garnered on CBCs were pished in (and most responded to the squeal call). No, I cannot say with certainty that some of those bird-eating raptors were not actually responding to the songbirds I'd attracted rather than to my vocalizations. Fine. Have it your way. I'm chumming for hawks.

But the fact is, I've watched Cooper's Hawks turn at the sound of a squeal call. (Ever notice that Cooper's Hawk have parabolic facial disks like owls and Northern Harriers? Don't tell me they don't hunt by sound.) I once had the same young and obviously very hungry female Cooper's Hawk land near me five times in a single afternoon—each time drawn to a squeal call.

Other raptors that have been snookered by the squeal call include Northern Harrier (many times, and males hunting brushy areas seem particularly gullible), Northern Goshawk, Red-shouldered Hawk (multiple times), Broad-winged Hawk, Red-tailed Hawk, Peregrine Falcon (the bird made a blind approach from across a marsh and landed in a nearby tree), and one Common Raven (an honorary raptor).

Owls are, of course, readily attracted to squeaking and squeals as demonstrated by how easily hunting Short-eared Owls can be turned during daylight hours (although they seem only gullible enough to be snookered once).

And other owls? Like Great Horned or Barred? Do they respond to squealing?

You must be joking. Only an idiot would go out and try and bait a Great Horned Owl with his face.

Is There Anything this Squeal Can't Do?

I've dedicated so much ink to uses for the squeal call readers must be wondering why birders would bother with any other vocal enticement. Two reasons. It's not universally well received (some birds turn the other way and go like hell when they hear it). And it's not easy to master.

But the squeal often works when all else fails, and it often incites reactions from birds that would not deign to respond to other forms of pishing.

Take marsh birds. The squeal call can get rails, gallinules, coots, and sometimes other marsh species to vocalize at night (in all fairness, though, clapping your hands or yelling can be equally effective).

Swallows massed for migration can be enticed to draw close in response to a prolonged bout of squealing (close enough to feel the wind of their wings, close enough to induce claustrophobia). On one very singular occasion I called in an Eared Quetzal while engaged in a bout of general pishing. It turns out that to the ears of this large bird of the Mexican mountain forests (and a very rare visitor to southeastern Arizona), the squeal call is not that dissimilar from the bird's loud, squealing *skreeee-chuck* call.

But birders who employ this call are very likely to enjoy close encounters of a furry and four-footed kind, as well, and I advise you to prepare for it. Many predatory animals find the call irresistible. Over the years, I have lured in dozens of foxes, several coyotes, three bobcats, one badger, any number of dogs, a few horses, several human hunters, and one game warden.

Harold Axtell told me that he once squeaked in a Striped Skunk. He encountered the animal while walking home from a lecture one night and, out of curiosity, started squealing. The animal approached slowly and, according to Harold, placed its nose on his shoe. When he stopped squealing, the skunk ambled away. When he started squealing again, the skunk returned and once again sought soulful intimacy with Harold's shoe.

I had a similar and slightly more intimate experience several years ago while scouting for the World Series of Birding (a twenty-four-hour contest held in New Jersey to see who can tally the most species) in the marshes near Tuckahoe. Hoping to entice a Sedge Wren to call, I started squealing and noticed a movement in the marsh grass that revealed itself to be a Short-tailed Weasel that ran directly toward me and stopped at my shoe. Somewhat taken aback by the animal's boldness, I stopped squealing. The animal responded by turning and moving off.

I don't get to see many weasels and Harold's story about the skunk had made an impression on me. I started to squeal again. Fast as a mirror can mimic, the agile predator turned and scampered back, but this time when he reached my shoe I continued squealing . . .

And was rewarded by having the animal run up my pants leg, stopping at about the point that the potential folly of this invitation became clear to me. But as soon as I stopped squealing, it turned, ran back down my leg, and bounded back into the marsh.

No harm done, and I'll never know for certain whether the animal would have continued to climb until he reached the source of the sound (my lips). Given the weasel's reputation for

The author being tutored in the art of loon identification by Roger Tory Peterson at the South Cape May Meadows during the first World Series of Birding competition. CHRIS STRUM

dogged determination and this one's obvious single-minded intent, I'll bet it would have.

To Pish or Not to Pish

Birds, like justice and cell phone service, are not evenly distributed across the planet. Even in bird-rich areas there are places of concentration and places of relative dearth. Needless to say, pishing is considerably less effective where there are no birds.

Even if you have lungs like bellows, lips of steel, impregnable bridgework, and jaw muscles that would engender envy in a pit bull, sauntering through the woodlands, pishing merrily as you go, is not an effective way of using your newly acquired gift for pishing. First, you won't be able to hear birds over the sound of your tolling, so you won't know where to stop and concentrate your efforts. Second, your ability to see bird movement will be masked by your own forward momentum. Third, no matter what your level of stamina, you can't pish forever. Being breathless and slack-jawed when it's time to bring your pishing skills to bear constitutes a bad strategy.

You are much better off marshaling your pish, employing it where there is strategic advantage, not squandering it in a vain, run-on hope. The best way to use your pishing skills is to walk quietly and attentively through woodlands or along a brushy edge. Listen for the call notes of birds. Move toward such birdy pockets. Position yourself strategically. Bring your binoculars to the ready.

Pish!

Pishing can also help you find birds. Try pausing every fifty or one hundred feet. Stop at places where you have encountered birds in the past or at places that seem birdy (a sunny, sheltered pocket on a cold and windy day) or a place that offers you strategic advantage (proximity to trees, nice overhanging branches, good light). Treat the place to about thirty seconds worth of boiler-plate pishing (nothing fancy) or a soft screech-owl warble or a thirty-second rendition of the pygmy-owl overture.

Most of the time, if there is a pish-piqued species within earshot, it will respond by vocalizing or approaching, letting you know that the place has potential. Where there is one bird, there are often more, and now that you have attracted a willing ally, the odds of drawing in more birds have just gone up.

There is one other occasion when I find pishing to be useful, and it is only indirectly related to finding birds. Like many people in the birding and natural history field, I frequently lead birding field trips, and sometimes birds are hard to come by. I've discovered that if you make a real good show of trying to find birds by enthusiastic pishing, people will be not only entertained but also more forgiving about your failure to show them birds.

Excuse my candor.

When NOT to Pish

It was early Sunday morning (early by most standards, but late for birders). My friend Greg Hanisek and I were standing in a suburban neighborhood street, scoping out bird feeders, trying to bolster our survey efforts as participants in the annual Hunterdon County Christmas Bird Count. Greg was the editor of the local paper (meaning he was a responsible sort). I work for New Jersey Audubon; I do socially redeemable things for a living. Neither of us is particularly rowdy or discourteous, and I felt confident that my very discrete pishing would never be heard by any of the residents still snug in their beds.

We didn't count on the dog—in fact, we never even heard the yappy little thing until a gentleman wearing boxer briefs and a frown opened the side door to his home and made a genuine and convincing effort to appear both put out and formidable.

"Christmas Bird Count," I explained. "Audubon Society," I added, invoking my diplomatic credentials.

But the gentleman was now both unamused and unappeased, and apparently had never signed an agreement according diplomatic immunity to Audubon Society representatives.

"You will cease this activity," he suggested, "or I will invoke my full rights as a citizen. Do I make myself *abundantly* clear?"

Clear enough. We apologized and left. And I've got to tell you that even though we got a kick out of the "abundantly clear" clause, and even though I'm pretty confident there are no ordinances specifically directed toward pishing on Sunday mornings, we knew that we were squarely in the wrong and felt pretty bad about disturbing the guy.

Let's be honest. Pishing is potentially annoying and disruptive, or, as Oliver Wendell Holmes might have phrased it, my power to pish my pish ends at the membrane across your ear canal. I don't like it when someone shows up in a natural area with a boom box cranked to max. But walking around hissing like a perforated steam pipe or whistling through a bolus of phlegm doesn't exactly add to the natural ambience either.

In many popular, well-birded areas, pishing is tacitly (if not actively) discouraged not only for aesthetic reasons but also because it can be disruptive and discourteous to others. One spring I was coleading a birding workshop. The group was split—some were with me, some were lingering back down the trail with the other leader. I started pishing and was rewarded by a Bicknell's Thrush that came barreling in and landed in plain sight, then leaving quickly.

When the other leader caught up, I gave her an enraptured account of our good fortune. She wasn't enchanted, and she wasn't surprised.

"I know," she related. "We were all trying to get a look at that bird, and when you started pishing, it bolted up here."

Oops.

In heavily birded places, particularly during peak season, go light on pishing. In fact, you might consider refraining altogether.

At other times, in other places, if you happen upon one or more birders, and they are working a nice little pocket, and you think that you might be able to pull a few good birds into the open with a surgical bout of pishing, ask whether anyone objects before tuning up.

In my experience, most people are delighted when an accomplished pisher works a bit of bird-attracting artistry, but this reaction is not universal. If anyone objects or even seems diffident, you have two choices: You can move on (and refrain from pishing until you are confident it won't interfere with their efforts), or you can wait until they leave.

While deference to birders should be axiomatic, courtesy to nonbirders who will have no idea what you are doing should be a priori.

I recall a few years ago my wife and I were birding southeastern Arizona, driving the little-used back way from Green Valley to Sonoita, when a bird flashed in front of the car. It was so long ago now that I forget what it was or what we hoped it might be. All I can tell you is that we skidded to a noisy halt (the road is dirt), jumped from the car, and started scanning the far side of an arroyo, pishing for all we were worth.

Only by slow degrees did we realize that we were not alone. Farther down the arroyo were two camera crews, two sound crews, twenty or so technicians, several actors, and one very impatient-looking director, all involved in shooting a scene for some new television series (the Young Riders, the Young Guns, the Young Outlaws . . . something like that), all with faces turned expectantly our way.

Calculated at union wage standards, my guess is that the interruption cost the show (and its sponsors) about ten thousand dollars. And we didn't even get the bird.

Oop$.

Taking Risks

Although courtesy and deference are excellent reasons to refrain from pishing, they pale in comparison to the very real danger that pishing may incur.

The risks inherent in trying to attract large and potentially dangerous birds of prey (such as Great Horned Owls) have already been mentioned. While I know of no cases where a birder has actually been struck or injured by a hawk or owl drawn to pishing, I can tell you from personal experience that I have been brushed more than once by Eastern Screech-Owls irked by my imitations of their calls. And there is one documented case of a person in Florida who was struck and injured by a Barred Owl while playing a recording of its call in the bird's territory.

Let me be clear, and let you be personally accountable. IF YOU ELECT TO ATTRACT BIRDS AND OTHER WILDLIFE BY ANY ORAL OR MECHANICAL MEANS, YOU ELECT TO ACCEPT A MEASURE OF PERSONAL RISK.

If you don't accept the risk, don't pish. Simple, no?

There are some places that you should simply *never* pish. One of them is bear country, particularly grizzly bear country. Almost any form of pishing might invite the curiosity of a bear, particularly a bear cub, which, after blundering into you, will undoubtedly let out a frightened bawl that will serve as your unhappy introduction to momma bear.

And the one thing you should absolutely, positively, never, ever, cross-your-heart-and-hope-to-god-you-die-quickly do is make a squeal call in dense habitat offering limited visibility. Or to frame this as a very plausible and illustrative birding scenario:

You and I are standing on a game trail in a large, mature willow thicket astride Alaska's Canning River. We are in the habitat of one of North America's rarest and most sought-after birds, the Gray-headed Chickadee. The area is also celebrated for its large numbers of grizzlies—North America's largest land carnivore.

And we can't see twenty feet. And you decide that you are going to try squealing—i.e., start sounding like a mortally wounded rabbit.

Not with me, buster. Good luck finding your chickadee. Make sure that your boots are laced and knotted (but it won't make any difference—griz can run faster than you can).

Risk Is as Risk Does

Although pishing involves an inherent risk to us, the greater risk is to birds, and while the risk is very small, it is real and should not be dismissed or ignored. Much of this risk can be minimized, or even eliminated, if birders behave intelligently and responsibly.

Pishing during that period of a bird's breeding cycle when young birds are in the nest or newly fledged is best avoided (across most of North America, this period falls between mid-May to mid-July—early August in more northern areas. At this time, adult birds are work stressed, and young birds are most vulnerable.

Use common sense. If you start pishing and a normally responsive but nondemonstrative adult towhee or woodpecker starts throwing an apoplectic fit, it's telling you that you've crossed the line. Shut up and back off.

On cold winter mornings, when temperatures are registering below about ten degrees, avoid pishing until birds have had a chance to feed and restore the energy stores they lost in their effort to survive the heat-leaching night. Don't make them waste energy by chasing phantom enemies for no greater reason than your own gratification.

This bit of insight was hard bought. In the opening chapter of my book *The Feather Quest*, I recount a birding adventure my wife and I had on a New Year's morning in the woodlands behind the house in North Jersey where I grew up. I describe an exciting and productive encounter with a mixed winter flock that included several Golden-crowned Kinglets and, very unexpectedly, a single Ruby-crowned Kinglet—a "half-hardy" species that the bitter cold temperatures should have removed from our reach. But they hadn't. Not quite.

What I did not mention was the fact that the kinglet arrived in a half-torpid state, weak from the cold and barely able to fly. We, of course, stopped pishing immediately, and I have every reason to believe that, without further distraction, the bird was able to forage successfully and maybe even survive what was a very cold winter for a bird north of its normal wintering range.

Birds are always trying to push the envelope this way. Upon reflection, I marvel, truly marvel, that weak as it was, that tiny little mite of a woodland bird was more eager to join the fracas than to feed. What a bird!

Another excellent time to refrain from pishing is when large numbers of migrating, bird-eating hawks are around. There are few places in North America where this is a concern. These are, for the most part, migratory concentration points and include such places as Cape May, New Jersey; Cape Charles, Virginia; and Whitefish Point, Michigan.

The peak of the migration for many songbirds corresponds to the peak migratory periods for many accipiters (forest hawks) and falcons (open-country hunters): April and early May in the spring, September and October in the fall. I have on two occasions I know of lured birds into the open that were, thus distracted, snatched by passing hawks. One of these birds, a Yellow-rumped Warbler, was snatched from a branch by a Sharp-shinned Hawk right in front of a workshop group.

If you are at this point thinking, "that's terrible," I quite agree with you. Nobody feels worse about the demise of that bird or any other bird that may have been killed indirectly by my distraction than I do.

But, to put this in perspective, I have been an avid pisher for thirty years. As such I played a part in two bird deaths. During this same period, I have killed more than thirty birds with my car (even though I'm really good at spotting birds, and my braking reflexes are pretty good). During this same period, somewhere between three hundred *million* and thirty *billion* birds have been killed as a result of fatally striking the windows of buildings (projections based on the work of Dr. Daniel Klem of Muhlenberg College).

For most bird species, ninety percent of all birds born in any single season fail to survive to the next. It's a real tough game of dice birds throw with the universe. But that doesn't mean that people like you and me, whose lives are entwined with birds', should be callous or uncaring about the great risks they take. And it certainly doesn't mean that we should, by our actions, mindfully or unmindfully increase those risks.

Pishing Contest

But should birders pish at all? Does the act of getting a bird's dander up inject unwarranted stress into its life?

Clearly, I don't think so, or I wouldn't be writing a book telling people how to do it. First off, birds have free will. They don't have to respond to pishing or to a mobbing action, and in fact, many times (for whatever reasons) they choose not to. If birds were biologically or psychologically hardwired to always respond to pishing no matter what I'd think differently about the matter. But birds clearly have a lot of latitude, and they vote with their wings.

Like Harold Axtell said: "Either they will be attracted, they will fly away, or they will do nothing."

By simple math, two out of three times they choose to blow you off. This sounds to me like a very sensible way of keeping stress levels under control. Speaking of which . . .

I'm of a mind that our culture obsesses about stress (or do I live in the only part of the country where every other TV commercial deals with sleep aids?). I'm certainly not trying to dismiss it or deny the fact that our society promotes an unhealthy level of stress. Heck, I'm the one trying to meet a book deadline here.

What I'm trying to say is that maybe my anxiety about my own miserable, stressed-out condition shouldn't be projected onto birds. Just because our species seems willing to run halfway to take stress by the hand doesn't mean that birds are so . . .

Or maybe they are. Maybe birds do choose to place themselves in stressful situations. The fact that they engage in mobbing behavior certainly supports this. So too does the act of establishing territories (that must be defended) or mobbing a roosting owl (that poses no threat).

The late Dr. Harold Axtell, birding sage and muse, who once observed that pishing will do one of three things: "It will attract birds. It will scare them away. Or it will do nothing."
PETE DUNNE

The fact is that stress is *natural,* and birds seem to handle it as a matter of everyday routine. And although inciting a mobbing action by pishing might be artificial, it is not unnatural.

But if you are really stressed about this issue, please, dear sir or madam, ponder the wisdom in this simple unassailable fact: We are dealing with professional birds here. They know what they are doing, so trust them to do what is in their best interest.

Fly toward you. Fly away from you. Do nothing.

Troubleshooting: Why Birds Do Nothing

Just as there are reasons why birds respond to pishing, there are reasons why they don't. Sometimes it can be for reasons already discussed.

You're too far from perches for birds to land on, or the forest where birds feel comfortable, or you are just too far from the bird itself. This is particularly true in the case of many canopy species. Hermit Warblers breed at the tops of mature western conifers (at heights that would induce a nosebleed in your average junco). You, standing at the base of that hundred-foot tree are just too insignificant to deal with.

Or you're wearing a bright, obvious, and intimidating color. Or it's too windy and the birds can't hear you (and you can't hear them). Or it's raining hard and the birds are under cover or it's too cold and the birds have their minds set on feeding or it's too hot and the birds are just too listless to deal with you. Or they're too tired because they were migrating all night and will be in the air again in a few hours.

One very common reason that birds do not respond to pishing is that they're too smart. These are birds that reside in heavily birded areas. They've heard it all and can probably identify every top pisher in North America by call in two seconds or less.

Let me tell you something, if you can manage to get any response more dramatic than a yawn out of a Carolina Chickadee in Cape May, you are one hell of a pisher.

It's akin to the story of the boy who cried wolf. After a bird falls for the ol' pishing ruse a few times and discovers that . . . Oh, it's only that Dunne bastard again . . . they wise up. They stop responding, or they stop responding enthusiastically.

Clearly not a place conducive to pishing.

You can test this yourself. Say you've got a territorial Prothonotary Warbler—a bird that normally responds well to pishing. You pish it up and get a great in-your-face response. The bird eventually loses interest and wanders off. If you wait a few minutes and try again, the bird might well respond again (but probably not as enthusiastically, and it probably will not remain as long).

The third time you try it, the bird may call but not approach, and if you try it a fourth time, chances are your efforts will be about as effective as pishing into the wind.

If you come back later in the day, or tomorrow, the bird may respond just as enthusiastically as the first time, but if this warbler is subjected to lots of pishing (as it might be in a heavily birded area) pretty soon it's going to ignore all these noisy people out there on the trail. The bird will become, as the term goes, "pished out."

Is this a bad thing? It's a matter of perspective. If you are a birder who has never seen a Prothonotary Warbler (and if you have not you owe it to yourself) it's a bad thing. But from the warbler's standpoint, it's simply a smart thing.

Many migrating songbirds clue in on the locals, join their feeding flocks, and do what they do (when in Rome, etc.). You could be the pishing equivalent of Top Gun, but if the local chickadees and nuthatches just roll their eyes and shake their heads when you unleash your blue ribbon pish, the visitors will follow suit.

By and large, pishing is most successful in late summer and fall, when bird populations are filled with new, young, and gullible birds. Immature birds are usually more responsive to pishing than adults. It could be lack of experience. It could be that young birds (like teenage humans) are just more cavalier.

This isn't anthropomorphic. Young hawks, for example, are far more likely to spar with each other during migration than adults are.

Pishing can also be very successful when birds are newly arrived on territory. Their hormones are pumping. They are territorial, defensive, quick to investigate anything potentially threatening within their domain.

But one of the main reasons birds do not respond to pishing is because they are a species that simply responds poorly, reluctantly, or not at all to pishing. These include most (but not all) nonperching birds, many flycatcher species, some wrens, some sparrows, and longspurs.

Nonpishable species. In the history of the world, no Laysan Albatross has ever responded to pishing.

In the long history of the world, nobody has ever pished in an albatross. Nobody has ever gotten a Black Swift to come in to squeaking. Spruce Grouse are impervious to *psssh, psssh, psssh.* In the pishing arena, it's a good practice to pick and choose the battles you can win.

Ten Easy Pishes

The flip side is that some species respond very well to pishing—bellwether birds. Focus on and practice on them. You'll get the reinforcing gratification you need to build confidence in your ability to attract birds. You'll be able to see what works for them and, just as importantly, for you.

Here's a list of ten widespread and easily pish-piqued species. At least some can be found in a habitat near you.

Downy Woodpecker. This common, widespread bird of small woodlots, arboreal suburban neighborhoods, parks, cornfields, even weedy fields is easily pish-piqued. It responds well

The small Downy Woodpecker is, for the most part, easy to provoke—in fact, it is sometimes the only bird to respond in bird-impoverished areas. But there are times when downies seem positively pish-proof, often when they are foraging in unforested habitats. KEVIN KARLSON

to the basic pish and the squeal. It treats a screech-owl call like a drink tossed in its face. It's found in pairs year-round, so the ire of one bird will almost certainly trigger a response in the other; you'll be facing pique in stereo. Other woodpecker species vary in their response to pishing. Some are very responsive, others are mostly unresponsive. None, however, is pish proof. Even the large Pileated Woodpecker will respond to the call of a larger owl (such as Barred Owl).

Great Crested Flycatcher responds quickly and vocally to pishing, but it may not necessarily leave the forest canopy. K.K.

Great Crested and Brown-crested Flycatchers. These woodland species respond very vocally to pishing and to owl calls (in fact, they pretty nearly erupt into a cacophony of sound). They commonly do not fly close but do respond quickly and tenaciously and serve as a bellwether for other forest birds. The Dusky-capped Flycatcher of extreme southeastern Arizona and southwestern New Mexico woodlands is also very vocal and very responsive to pishing. The more common and widespread Ash-throated Flycatcher, a bird of more open, brushy areas, is somewhat less responsive. It may investigate your overtures to engage in a harangue, but it often elects to sit on the sidelines.

Red-eyed Vireo. Even though this species forages in the canopy and subcanopy, it responds quickly to almost any form

Red-eyed Vireo can be coaxed from the tops of trees, and its scold call seems to get other forest species' danders up. K.K.

of pishing, lending its own descending, nasal, whiny scold call to your vocal array. In summer and during migration, if you are trying to jump-start a mobbing action, this species should be one of the first picks for a pishable all-star team. In fall, even when nothing else is responding, you can almost always get one of these common birds to give you an audience. Other responsive vireos include White-eyed, Philadelphia, Warbling, Bell's, Hutton's, Yellow-throated, Plumbeous, Cassins, and Blue-headed.

Blue Jay. This one blows hot and cold. It can at times respond to pishing as quickly and forcefully as a SWAT team. At other times it appears timorous and reluctant to approach (even after you have its attention). But once you've succeeded in triggering a mobbing action, Blue Jays seem to be unable to resist getting into the fray. At the very least, their excited, loud

The Blue Jay is easily provoked by a screech-owl imitation, but it's usually one step behind the pack when mobbing action is incited; it responds more to the mob than to you. Once drawn, however, the jay's scolding cries act like a clarion call to other, more retiring species. K.K.

braying will alert all other able-bodied birds within earshot that the militia is mustering. The western Steller's Jay is somewhat less responsive (the generally greater height of western trees might have something to do with this). It may be vocal, but it commonly keeps its distance. The Green Jay of Texas is reticent, and Scrub Jays, though attentive, are also somewhat aloof. The similar but more geographically restricted Mexican Jay of southeastern Arizona, southwestern New Mexico, and (barely) the Big Bend corner of Texas, is more responsive. The widespread but northern Gray Jay can be very responsive to pishing but, in truth, if you just stand in Gray Jay habitat, the intensely bold and curious birds will come over to investigate without prompting.

Tufted Titmouse. Tied with Black-capped and Carolina Chickadees for top honors in the Pish America contest. Even the most basic *psssh, psssh, psssh* seems to get a rise out of this crested, ankle-biting little terrier of a bird. Even Aunt Mabel's most timorous cat-calling effort might send this common woodland and suburban species into a stuttering rage. Other titmice, except for the Black-crested Titmouse of Texas, are less blatantly responsive but are still fairly easily tweaked. Try a basic pish–small owl combination and a bit of patience.

A common woodland species, Tufted Titmouse is runner-up in the most-pishable competition, and possibly the bird whose scold call is the foundation of the basic pish. K.K.

The Pish King. When you hear Black-capped Chickadees, pish! They come in quickly, usually in a stuttering rage, and other species will follow. k.k.

Black-capped, Carolina, and Mountain Chickadees. These three species are pishable to the nth degree. Boreal, Mexican, and Chestnut-backed Chickadees are slightly less hair-triggered but pishable nevertheless. Common within their respective ranges, these species, like Tufted Titmouse, will respond to all manners of vocal tweaking. The first notes of a screech-owl warble often send black-caps into a stuttering rage, and their responsiveness is matched by their tenacity. Mick Jagger's classic "Start Me Up" might well have been written about chickadees.

Bushtit. This tiny western and southwestern pack animal is both common and widespread in brushy or wooded areas but may be somewhat timorous and slow to respond to pishing. Be

A common western species, Bushtits travel in packs and will cross open areas to investigate a pish-provoked ruckus. They usually take a bit of coaxing but rarely fail to respond. K.K.

patient and persistent because, once activated, these birds weave a defensive little tapestry of darting forms and spitting scolds. In the West, you always want a pack of Bushtits on your side. It helps to gain and hold the attention of more pish-resistant species.

The Verdin, a small, titlike bird of arid desert brushland, is more reticent than Bushtit but is nevertheless among your pishable best bets in this harsh habitat (and it commonly comes in pairs). Once you've triggered this bird's rapid chipping, you might encourage Black-tailed Gnatcatchers or, especially, Bewick's Wrens to join in.

A chunky wind-up toy of a bird, the White-breasted Nuthatch responds quickly and tenaciously to almost any form of pishing and often seems more curious than piqued. K.K.

White-breasted Nuthatch. A widespread, year-round resident primarily of hardwood forests, easily piqued by pishing and tenacious when provoked. It is also quite fearless, often approaching closely and imparting confidence to more timid species that might otherwise hang back. It responds particularly well to a combination of screech-owl and basic pish. Several other nuthatch species (Red-breasted, Pygmy, and Brown-headed) are slightly less easily stimulated than the larger White-breasted, but, in some respects, they are even more tenacious when it comes to dishing out admonishments. Pygmy and Brown-headed Nuthatches are pack animals. The members of the group seem to egg one another on, prolonging the response.

Yellow-rumped Warbler, a common northern breeder and a flocking species in winter, will descend from treetops and respond from great distances to investigate a well-orchestrated bout of pishing. K.K.

Yellow-rumped Warbler. In truth, several other warbler species are just as easily pish-piqued as this one (most notably Yellow and Black-and-White Warblers and American Redstart), and, with few exceptions, warblers in general are very responsive to pishing. It's just that Yellow-rumped Warblers (both the eastern Myrtle form and the western Audubon's) are widespread northern breeders, common migrants across virtually all of North America, and found as winter residents across much of the South and coastal United States. Since they migrate and winter in flocks, they are emboldened by their numbers and respond quickly and tenaciously to almost any form of pishing.

Try larding a screech-owl or Saw-whet or Northern Pygmy-Owl imitation into the basic pish. Yellow-rumps (and warblers in general) also respond very well to chips.

Fox Sparrow. Many sparrow species (particularly woodland and edge species) respond well to pishing, but the four populations of Fox Sparrow are widespread—northern and western woodland breeders common across the southern coastal United States in winter. Song Sparrows are actually more common and more widespread and generally respond more immediately to pishing—but not as vigorously. They often key up and then just sit there. Fox Sparrows, once piqued, are bold, vocal, and tenacious, and other species (juncos, towhees, other sparrows) seem to take their loud, admonishing chip notes seriously.

The widespread woodland Fox Sparrow can be slow to respond to pishing. But once activated—and once you have five or six birds keyed up atop a nearby bush—you can hardly get Fox Sparrows to leave. K.K.

4 | Beyond Pishing

Most birds respond to sound (why else would they vocalize?), and pishing covers only one band (albeit broad) of the audio spectrum. There are other audio enticements—some vocal, some percussive—that birders can use to attract birds or, at the very least, prompt them to disclose their presence. Here are a few of my favorites.

Imitation

I am forever amazed at how quickly birds respond to even poor imitations of their own vocalizations and songs. Orioles must rank among the planet's most gifted vocalists, and the Baltimore Oriole is a practiced Pavarotti among them. But if you can whistle "shave and a haircut, two bits" (in any key), you can probably get a Baltimore Oriole to take up the challenge and play "now top this" with a whistled response of its own.

Virtually anyone who can whistle can entice Northern Bobwhite to engage in a duet, and in spring and summer a territorial Yellow-breasted Chat ranks among the planet's more easily piqued and imitated birds. You don't even have to match the bird's considerable vocal array. Just two or three different well-spaced whistled phrases sandwiched between admonishing squeaks and stuttering *shh*s are usually enough to make the birds go ballistic, literally.

The rowing winged flight display of a chat is comically expressive.

The calls of many shorebird species are easily mimicked, and even high-flying shorebirds can be seduced from the sky. Have you ever seen that famous painting by Thomas Eakins *Whistling for Plover?* It depicts a young, intense African American hunter (in a straw hat and white shirt) crouched in an open marsh with his double-barreled shotgun at the ready and his lips pursed in a telltale pucker.

The fact that the dead and crippled birds around him are Greater Yellowlegs, which are sandpipers, not plovers, does not diminish the drama of the painting or my point. Fact is, the whistled calls of both Greater and Lesser Yellowlegs, as well as Black-bellied Plovers, are very easy to imitate, and all three species respond well to them. (By the way, in all fairness to Eakins, at the time the Philadelphia painter was laying brush to canvas, Greater Yellowlegs were widely, if inaccurately, called Yellow-legged Plovers.)

The way I try to get Virginia (and King) Rails to vocalize during the World Series of Birding is to bring my fingers to my mouth (as if I were going to squeal) but position my lips closer to my hand (not in the middle of the finger) and make a series of low-pitched, sucking-quacking notes in a quickening and descending pattern that replicates the birds' calls. Usually my effort is horrible. But rails are forgiving and often respond, just as they sometimes do to any loud sound, such as the clapping of hands.

My World Series teammate Don Freiday does a wonderful imitation of the drum of a Ruffed Grouse. He accomplishes this feat by cupping his hands and thumping on his chest in the percussive bouncing-ball-rolling-to-a-stop pattern of a drumming grouse: *Thump . . . Thump . . . ThumpThumpThumpThump-Th'Th'Th'Th'ThThTh'h'h'h'h'thump.*

It works, too. I know several grouse and one rival Big Day team that have fallen for it.

And what Big Day team does not know the old striking-two-quarters-together trick? It's a great way to ensure that a team a hundred yards away will be able to count Yellow Rail on their list (thanks to your imitation), and, who knows?, it might even get a real Yellow Rail to call for you. Although some woodpeckers (such as Northern Flickers) vocalize, most post notice of their territorial boundaries by drumming—hammering on wood in a species-specific pattern. Downy Woodpeckers have a short drum sequence of notes that is slow enough to count, given at frequent intervals—every ten to fifteen seconds. A sapsucker's pattern begins with a short, strong, rapid series of drums that slows and breaks into a halting pattern at the end. You can imitate these different drumming patterns by banging a sturdy stick against a handy resonant tree and get real territorial woodpeckers to respond by drumming or flying in to see their presumed rival.

There are, among the ranks of birders, some who are incredibly gifted—able to imitate birdsong so accurately that even the birds themselves might find it difficult to emulate. I know a Connecticut birder whose rendering of a Winter Wren song is so good that it would take an acoustics laboratory to distinguish it from the real thing.

Striving to imitate the songs, calls, and other communication efforts of birds can be a fun, challenging, and often rewarding endeavor. Succeed or fail, it is, at the very least, a way of increasing your awareness of bird sounds and the important role they play in both finding and identifying birds.

All too often birders come to this wisdom late in their birding careers. Some never discover it.

Pish Poor

I have a friend (let's call him Bob) who is a very skilled birder and who is, still, after these many years, about the worst pisher I have ever met. His screech-owl sounds like an asthmatic canary. His Barred Owl makes people cringe. His long, loud, juicy, and regimented standard pish sequence suggests the last, flatulent, gasps of a deflating truck tire mired in a puddle.

But he seems genially undaunted by this. And, as often happens, when birds are in a forgiving mood, they give him the benefit of the doubt.

Some of you, like Bob, might be pish challenged and you may at this point be thinking, I can't do this.

Yes, you can, because *can* manifests itself in degrees.

Look, do you think St. Francis was a born pisher? Do you think that one morning, just after matins, he walked out of the cloister, opened up his arms, shouted *"Pishio!"* and birds rained down like feathered manna? Not likely. Pishers are no more born than are saints, and if it came down to one or the other, your chances of becoming a proficient pisher are probably greater than your mustering the requisite number of miracles to get canonized.

What's more, you can enjoy the fruits of pishing while you're still alive. Canonization demands that you be dead. So while you are on this side of the void, concentrate and polish the bird-attracting sounds you can make—the basic pish, the back-of-your-thumb squeal. There are lots of birds that can be coaxed into a response by these two basic sounds. Some of them are probably within walking distance of where you are right now.

In the local park. In your own backyard. Go hunt up a chickadee. It won't bite. It won't laugh. It won't hold a grudge. It . . .

Will probably surprise you how quickly the bird will respond to your whispered overtures. Curious or piqued, it will certainly give you its full attention (have you ever locked eyes with something as animate and alive as a bird? It's almost communion) and, chances are, given the fact that it is a chickadee, it will probably call in a few friends.

And always remember, sometimes pishing doesn't work no matter how accomplished a pisher you are. So what. Who cares? Birding in general is a low-stakes game. If a bird ignores your overtures, nations don't fall, currencies don't collapse, children don't starve. It's a low-stakes game where you can only win (you get a close and satisfying look at a bird) and you can't lose.

By the way, did I mention that in order for pishing to work you need to have a pure heart?

Oh.

Well, you need a pure heart.

But Aren't There Some Things That . . . Well, You Know, Things You Can Buy?

Yes, there are things you can buy, over-the-counter devices that make it possible for people experiencing pishing dysfunction to get the same effect. The Audubon Bird Call is one such device.

It's a small, cork-sized chunk of birch wood with a twisting, metal hooky-dooky stuck on the top that, when given a quarter turn, produces a squeak or chirp that is almost identical to the squeak call made by kissing your fingers.

Sold in many stores and nature centers catering to the bird-watching trade, the calls will set you back about ten dollars—which is pretty expensive for something that has one moving part and produces a sound you can manufacture by kissing your fingers.

But if it gets you a look at a Connecticut Warbler—priceless.

A squeal call, perhaps the hardest sound to master, can also be purchased. Go into almost any sporting goods store catering to the hook-and-bullet crowd and buy a predator call. The squealing is designed to replicate the sound of a wounded rabbit, but it closely resembles a wounded starling too.

You can also carry a CD player (or cassette player, if they are still being manufactured by the time this book hits the racks). Slip in a CD of North American birdsongs. Punch in the number that corresponds to "Screech-Owl, Eastern." Hit "Repeat." Walk around with the sound of Eastern Screech-Owl blaring.

And if I meet you, I'll have to kill you.

While there is nothing inherently wrong with using play-back recordings, the temptation to overuse them is immense, and many people seem unable to resist. In the hands of professional tour guides, who use playbacks to judiciously entice birds into the open where they can be easily seen by a group, a CD player is a great tool. It is, in many respects, more surgical and less overtly disrupting than pishing, because playback recordings are most commonly directed at individual species, whereas pishing is broadband—most often used to incite whatever might be hiding in the vicinity.

A few years ago, my pishing skills were employed as part of a regional survey that sought to establish the amount of use that designated areas were getting by migrating birds. The protocol called for surveyors to go to prescribed spots, hit the play button, bombard the area with three minutes of my prerecorded pishing, and note any birds that came in. They had to do this for weeks.

What did the survey prove? It proved that pishing unfettered by the self-limiting mechanisms imposed by the human condition (finite lung capacity, lactic acid buildup in jaw muscles, phlegm reserve depletion) is about as endearing as a case of shingles.

Look, I know there is a CD that goes with this book. I know that you can take it in the field and call in birds. But that would defeat the purpose. The whole point of this book is to empower *you* to go into the field and use your own skills to engage birds. By using a CD to attract birds, you would be undercutting the importance of skill and devaluing success.

You are also putting yourself at grave risk. Because scattered among ranks of birders are recovering researchers. People who, only now, are beginning to lead normal lives, having finally purged their minds of the sound of my pishing. You won't know them just to see them. They look as normal as you and I. But if they were to hear the sound of my pishing again, and they realize it's coming from you, there is no telling what they might do.

On Birding

This may seem like a funny place to begin to explain the greater activity that pishing is merely a part of. But it might be that you picked up this book thinking that the subject matter related to something else, or, more likely, you are just some-body who likes birds and thought it might be nice to learn how to talk to them.

If you fall into either of these categories then you undoubt-edly realize by this time that your initial premise was either misguided or false. But now that you've gotten this far, perhaps you've become somewhat curious to know more about the arcane activity that spawned a book dedicated to so much obscure lore.

That would be bird-watching, or birding, North America's fastest-growing (and second-largest) outdoor activity.

The growing popularity of birding is rooted in several things, including the suburbanization of America, the growing number of retirees (particularly younger, active retirees), and a very large, diverse, and healthy bird population. The only rea-son this is worth mentioning is because if you suddenly find yourself interested in going birding, you can rest assured that you are far from alone.

There are two things you need to do to be a birder: You need to find birds, and you need to find out what they are—i.e., you need to identify them. It's like a treasure hunt. When you find and pin the right name to a bird, you cast a binding spell on it. You make it yours to keep in the coffers of your mind.

You also get to spend lots of time outdoors, meet a lot of great people, and see a lot of spectacular country both here and abroad. There are about eight hundred species of birds in North America, ten thousand in the world. If you are starting now, you have a lot of fun and a lot of challenge ahead of you.

There are two pieces of equipment that you will need to help you find and identify birds. The first is a pair of binoculars, which vault distances, making it possible to see the traits that distinguish one bird species from another. You will also need a field guide, a book that both depicts birds (in photos or illustrations) and provides other useful hints and clues that will help you locate and identify species.

There are a goodly number of binoculars, ranging in price from fifty dollars to two thousand dollars, that are designed to meet the demands of birding. That's the good news. The bad news is that for every one pair that work for birding, there are ten that do not. *The biggest problem beginning birders face is that they have the wrong binoculars and don't realize it.*

Unless you go to a store that specializes in meeting the needs of birders, or unless you meet other birders and see what they are using, chances are you are going to buy the wrong binoculars. Look, I run two nature centers. I lead lots of birding field trips. I see this happening to beginning birders all the time.

Try this. Go online. Key in www.njaudubon.org. Click on CMBO (for Cape May Bird Observatory). Click on "Pick of the Pack." You'll find a short summary of binocular makes and models that are appropriate for birding. But there is still no guarantee that any particular model will work for you. The only sure way to find binoculars that meet your specific needs is to go someplace where you can test them personally. Pick a few favorites from the list, find a store near you, and test and compare.

There are considerably fewer field guides on the market—none without merit—but some are nevertheless better suited than others for beginners. My heartfelt recommendation is that you pick up Kenn Kaufman's *Birds of North America* or Roger

Tory Peterson's *Birds of Eastern and Central North America* (or the companion book *Western Birds*). I also heartily recommend that you purchase the *Sibley Guide to Birds* by David Allen Sibley because of its simple excellence.

How about my own books on bird watching? Nah. That would be too self serving.

Pssst! Last Words

Congratulations. You have mastered the course. The only assignment left is to take the pledge and be welcomed into the Order of Pishers. Use your gift frugally but well. Have a ball. Impress your neighbors, win friends, and influence people. After all, if more people become intimate with birds, they will become more interested in and protective of them. Which means that they will necessarily become protective of the habitat that sustains birds (because no habitat, no birds). And this means . . .

They'll vote green. Something that St. Francis, and I, heartily approve.

One last thing. In case you harbor any lingering doubts about the effectiveness of pishing, be consoled by this unassailable wisdom:

Even if all the rude, obnoxious and embarrassing noises that constitute pishing have no effect whatsoever upon birds, the act of pishing still forces a person to stand in one spot for an extended period of time. And over most of the globe, if you stand in a place long enough, a bird is sure to appear.

Did I mention that you need a pure heart?

I thought I might have.

Pisher's Pledge

On my honor
I will do my best
For birds and birding
To pish with gusto
And a rising inflection
But not conduct myself
In a manner that puts birds at risk
Or causes angst
To birders and nonbirders alike
So help me Pish.

CD Track Listings

1 Basic pish
Pish variation
Pish with a stutter

2 Eastern Screech-Owl warble
Eastern Screech-Owl whinny

3 Barred Owl call
Northern Saw-whet Owl call
Northern Pygmy-Owl call

4 Basic call sequence review
Squeal
Simple chip
Sequential chip

5 Whisper pish

6 Knockdown pish

7 Pishing etiquette